Best Wishes

this

Holiday Season

from

Bank of Marin

POINT REYES
VISIONS

**PHOTOGRAPHS AND ESSAYS
POINT REYES NATIONAL SEASHORE
AND WEST MARIN**

POINT REYES
VISIONS

**PHOTOGRAPHS AND ESSAYS
POINT REYES NATIONAL SEASHORE
AND WEST MARIN**

**PHOTOGRAPHS BY RICHARD P. BLAIR
TEXT BY KATHLEEN P. GOODWIN**

COLOR & LIGHT EDITIONS
Inverness, California

FERNS AND BAY TREE
Bear Valley Trail

FRONTISPIECE: Sword ferns on the Bear Valley Trail, 1973

First Edition

ISBN 0-9671527-4-7

Printed in Singapore

TREES ON INVERNESS RIDGE
From Elephant Mountain

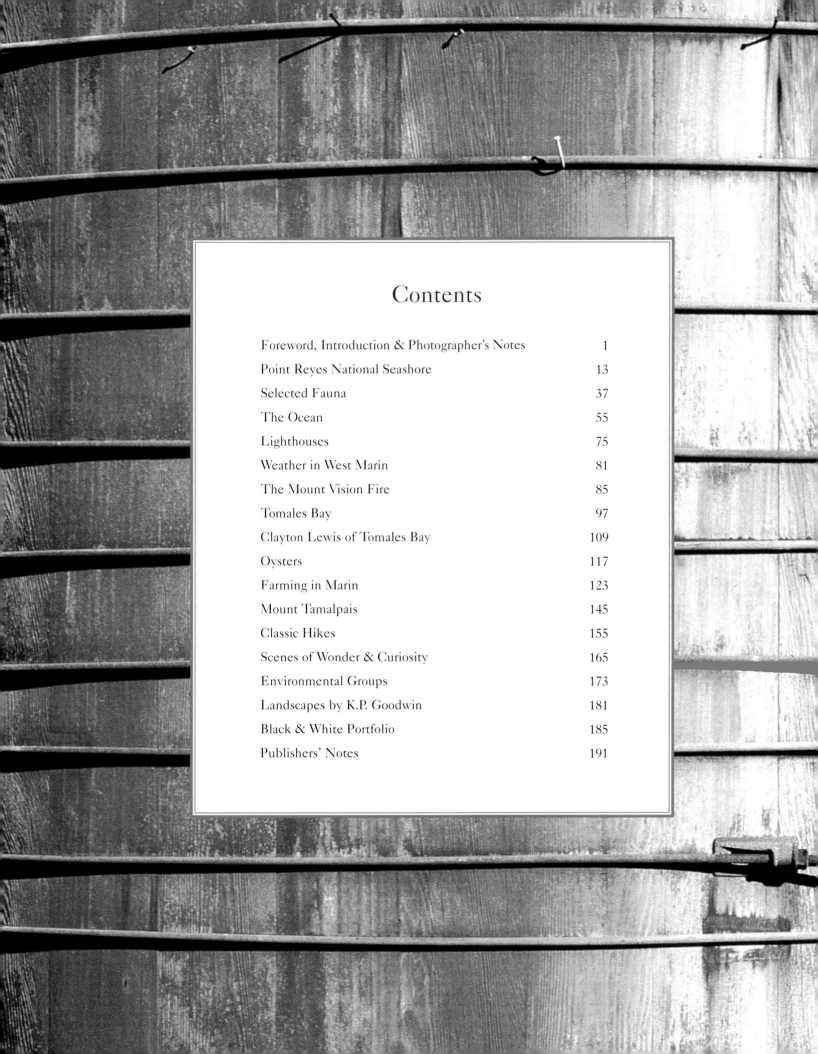

Contents

FOREWORD

Throughout my life I have migrated to wild places on America's coast-lines. I have lived and worked in Alaska, northern California, and on the east coast in various wild places. As a child, I hiked and camped throughout California in such phenomenal places as Yosemite and Lassen National Parks. Eventually, Point Reyes and West Marin became my home, a coastal wilderness sanctuary with special magic.

Over the last 20 years, I have explored the entire Point Reyes Peninsula, from the backcountry trails to other secret places. I have grown to fully appreciate how wild this peninsula remains. Almost every hike leads to an incredible view of a bobcat, whale, or a spectacular wildflower – and the rebirth of my spirit. These experiences keep me inspired and alive.

One of my favorite places is Tomales Point. As one hikes out this northern tip of the peninsula the Pacific Ocean can be viewed to the west and Tomales Bay can be seen to the east. On a spring day, the area is covered by a carpet of Douglas iris and other wildflowers and elk graze on verdant grasses. On a fall day, one can hear the bugling of the bull elk, trying to herd their harem. I feel this area is the epitome of wildness.

From my perspective, Point Reyes is paradise, a treasure now saved for generations to come. My hope is that future generations will find the passion many of us have for ensuring its magnificent qualities are preserved forever.

Richard Blair and Kathleen Goodwin are passionate artists and environmentalists. Richard's sepia photograph of the Headlands graces my home. I hope that their photography and writing will intro-duce you to a deeper relationship with Point Reyes National Seashore.

DON NEUBACHER

Don is currently the Superintendent of the Point Reyes National Seashore. He has worked for the National Park Service in Alaska, the Golden Gate National Recreational Area and the Denver Service Center.

AERIAL VIEW OF POINT REYES LIGHTHOUSE, CHIMNEY ROCK AND DRAKES BAY.

ELEPHANT MOUNTAIN AT DAWN
Aerial taken over Olema Hill looking north
PHOTOGRAPH BY K.P. GOODWIN

INTRODUCTION

Getting to know West Marin for me was like coming home. I was born in South Africa and lived there until I was a young adult. After I moved to the Bay Area, I missed South Africa's wide open spaces. Then I discovered West Marin. It filled a need to rest my eyes on expansive beauty. There were trails where I could walk for miles with opportunities to come across animals and birds living in their natural habitat.

Point Reyes National Seashore became my place of escape with its coastal forests, fresh air, foggy beaches and abundant wild life. During the 25 years I have lived in the Bay Area, I hiked, camped and swam there.

One of my favorite hikes is out to Chimney Rock. On one side is Drakes Bay; on the other is the Pacific Ocean and the sound of elephant seals barking. In the distance is the faint outline of San Francisco. Sometimes the ocean is pounding and clouds are threatening. There is a wildness in the wind and it is easy to imagine the ancient ships being wrecked off the shore. In the springtime Chimney Rock is covered with wildflowers, a vision of yellow, blue and occasional red.

The summer fog brings moisture in an otherwise very dry season and enables forests of bishop pine and Douglas fir to flourish. The forests in Point Reyes vary from the lush forest with its closed canopy on the Bear Valley trail to the drier more open woods along the ridges of Mount Vision and Mount Wittenberg.

Walking along the ocean south of Drakes Beach, the rust colored cliffs with the huge sand dunes and wind eroded forms brings to mind a desert. If you look towards the sea, there is rich life among the tide pools, pelicans flying overhead and the occasional seal observing hikers from beyond the breakers.

This area is a rare treasure.

KATHLEEN P. GOODWIN

FEATHER AND THE SEA
Kehoe Beach

PHOTOGRAPHER'S NOTES

The initial attraction of Point Reyes for us were the beaches of Drakes Bay, Limantour Beach and, and the trail to Coast Camp. There we connected with the ocean and with a part of California that was still agrarian and laid back.

The first conversation Kathleen and I ever had was in a Berkeley cafe. I told her about the afternoon I had just spent watching pelicans fly over my head at Tomales Point at the very top of the Point Reyes Seashore. She was eager to see this magical place I described. It was the beginning of our relationship.

We lay hidden in the high grass on a cliff south of Limantour Beach, with a grand view of the rollicking waves. Full of joy, we ran down to the beach, like true Californians do, in a ritual dance of free–falling, bounding and sliding down the little canyon that led to the beach and water. I found myself running out of control. Suddenly the trail stopped at a small but unforeseen cliff and I was flying though the air. I somersaulted, landing flat on my bare back in a soft bed of stinging nettles whose leaves had hundreds of tiny thorns. I ended up in the Kaiser Emergency room that evening being treated by the doctor who suggested that that the way to get rid of the thorns was to lift them from my skin with masking tape, a procedure I do not recommend.

Since being a boy scout in the Bronx (it was wild once!), I have ventured as far afield as possible, leading many hikes and climbs. I was park photographer at Yosemite in the 70's. I have always supported myself with my camera and am grateful that the medium of photography allows me to combine my love of art and exploration.

To learn about our *modus operandi*, please refer to Publishers Notes at the end of the book where we discuss our production methods, open studio events and workshops.

Thanks to all the people who helped and encouraged us.

RICHARD BLAIR

POINT REYES NATIONAL SEASHORE is many things: bays flanked by white cliffs, undulating farmlands, miles of pristine beaches, forested ridges and valleys with fingers of fog weaving in and out, birds and animals appearing with startling frequency.

While some national parks are natural architectural wonders, Point Reyes is rather a Japanese haiku. It is the

region, a mountain lion is living, adds an edge to hiking which I value.

Writing about national parks is, for us, like writing about religion. Parks are our churches where we worship the wilds. In a problematic world, to have special reserves of land where nature can flourish is perhaps as close as we can get to Eden.

SUNSET TOWARD ELEPHANT ROCK
South of McClures Beach

antidote for people over stimulated by modern detail. The landscapes are severely long and horizontal with a simple beauty which sneaks up on you. Its changeable weather brings painterly collusions of light and form.

An extensive trail system gives hikers freedom to find their own hidden spot. Some trails are seldom frequented and it is possible to hike for hours only seeing birds and animals. For me, the knowledge that somewhere in the

Point Reyes National Seashore, with its proximity to San Francisco, poetically complements the foggy sophisticated metropolis. The beaches of Point Reyes are also cool and grey in the fog. They are wilderness areas for visitors who appreciate miles of lonely beaches, the smell of a fresh breeze off the ocean rather than the aroma of cotton candy. These isolated beaches, coves and headlands are amazingly pristine. No amusement park rides like big city beaches here. Instead animals and plants abound in a landscape deeply resistant to human change.

The prevailing westerly winds direct nutriment rich waters to our coast, creating vast food reserves for marine life: salmon, seals, sea lions and the great white shark. The nearest land mass, the coast of Asia, is half a world away, yet we share the edge of the Pacific, the longest edge on the earth.

Point Reyes is constantly observed by satellites, seismographs and in park research laboratories, but what is known of the park's real secrets? The relationships of nature are infinite in complexity. We humans need to participate in wild environments, where the mysteries of life, death and nature are before us. We use the fresh perspective to renew ourselves. In wilderness we share our planet with all the other species. We hear but cannot understand bird calls, elephant seal rumblings, the scream of mountain lions, these inhuman voices of our hereditary neighbors, but we can feel their wild hearts.

MALE ELEPHANT SEAL

Wind and fog, wind and fog. Ancient forests of Bishop Pine, Douglas Fir, dripping, fading in and out of view as clouds race by... fog pouring over a ridge 1407 feet high at Mt Wittenberg... Ocean water rhythmically breaks on rocks and sand, creates the primal alliance and primal opposition of water with shore.

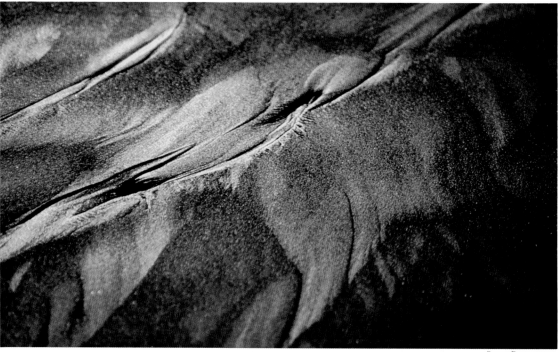

SAND PATTERNS
Sculptured Beach

A VERY BRIEF HISTORY

The earth's crust slides along the San Andreas fault pushing north this sliver of granite rock, Point Reyes, floating on a sea of molten rock. Ice ages have come and gone. Man crossed the frozen Bering Sea increasing his range to the Americas. Man, the tool user, built ships. Sir Francis Drake circumnavigated, landing on the shore of Point Reyes in 1579. Chinese pottery dated to the late 1570's confirm a Drakes Bay landing site.

THE COAST MIWOK INDIANS

Drake was greeted by a friendly tribe of Coast Miwoks living in the area.He wrote in his diary that he travelled into the interior (towards present day Novato!) and visited several substantial Coast Miwok villages with over 300 inhabitants. Each had a permanent ceremonial building in the center of the village. Their homes were built of redwood bark in the cone shape of tepees and could stand for 60 years. Smaller less permanent buildings, lasting about five years, were made with a frame of willow in the shape of a modern dome tent. Tule reeds were attached to the framework with rope made from fronds of the tule reed.

The Coast Miwoks had been living in the area for thousands of years. Stone tools including an ax made from chert, have been found on the peninsula. They have been carbon dated to be between 5 and 10,000 years old. A 5,000 year old abalone trading shell from Point Reyes was found on the western mud flats of the Mississippi River. The Coast Miwoks also lived in smaller family encampments along Tomales Bay and throughout West Marin. It was a comparatively easy life, the climate temperate, plenty of fish, shellfish and game for hunting. The inhabitants were not warlike and many consider this was the reason they lost their land so quickly to the Europeans.

KULE LOKLO

Near the park headquarters at Bear Valley, is Kule Loklo, a replica of a Coast Miwok village. It has a sweat lodge, a dance house, tepee shaped structures, (known as kotcas), built of redwood bark and willow and tule reed, and shade arbors. It is used by local Indians for religious ceremonies and family reunions. Twice a year the Federated Coast Miwoks hold gatherings at Kule

HUT OF WILLOW & TULE REED
Kule Loklo

REDWOOD BARK KOTCA
Kule Loklo

Loklo; the third Saturday in July is Big Time, a trade feast similar to a flea market and on the fourth Saturday in April is the Strawberry Festival which features dancing exhibitions. Basket weaving, arrowhead making and other traditional California Indian skills are taught at Kule Loklo in workshops organized by the Miwok Archeological Preserve of Marin.

EARLY COLONIZATION

The Spanish colonized Mexico and California. Trade routes were established. Russians traded pelts at Jenner. Priests built missions, including, in 1817, the Mission San Rafael where local Indians were brought to live. In 1835 the Mexican government secularized the missions, and the Indians were left to fend for themselves. Some died from disease, others tried to return to their old life but often their land was taken by the European settlers. In 1846 the American government gained control of California. When gold was discovered in 1849, the new state boomed. Many of the old land grants were acquired by litigious lawyers, who then leased the land to dairy farmers. Cows thrived eating Point Reyes grasslands, and the butter produced was prized by San Franciscans who were building Victorian houses with coastal redwoods. After the great earthquake of 1906 they built again. On the ridge, hunting clubs were built. Teddy Roosevelt hunted at Divide Meadow. Bears were hunted to extinction.

SAN FRANCISCO & THE GOLDEN GATE
View from Marin Headlands

WIND AND SUN ON BEACH GRASSES
Limantour Spit

It is almost unprecedented in this country that such a long stretch of land so close to a city the size of San Francisco, would be left practically in its natural state. It was the outcome of a combination of luck, foresight and hard work. In 1851, the land just north of the Golden Gate was acquisitioned by the US Army. This protected it from urban development for over a century. When changes in technology rendered these fortifications ineffectual after WW II, the area was available for parkland. Further north, the National Park Service proposed, in 1935, the purchase of 53,000 acres of land in Point Reyes,

then available for $2.4 million. Unfortunately the acquisition of public land, for what was considered a huge amount of money, was not popular and the deal did not go through. Drakes Beach and McClures Beach were set aside as county parks. It was not until 1962 that the Point Reyes National Seashore Bill was signed by President John F. Kennedy, authorizing the creation of the 53,000 acre preserve. Clem Miller, a California congressman, was a key park advocate. The U.S. Congress set aside $13 million for the task. Three years later the money had been spent and less than half the land within the boundaries of the park had been acquired. The area meanwhile was increasing in value. The Park Service considered selling some of its parkland to developers

POINT REYES HEADLANDS & DRAKES BAY, SUNSET
View from Inverness Ridge

SLEEPING SEA LION

so that it could acquire other land considered more essential.

In response to this new threat, Marin conservationists, led by Marin County supervisor, Peter Behr, formed an organization called "Save Our Seashore". They started a petition asking for the preservation of the entire park and half a million people signed it. On November 19, 1969 congress designated sufficient money to acquire the rest of park at a cost of $56 million. Its range includes coastal mountains, wetlands, beaches, lakes, dams, lagoons, estuaries, bays, pasture lands. It protects the sites of Miwok buildings and middens and offers sanctuary to thousands of different species of animals, insects, birds, plants, trees and flowers.

In 1971 Congressman Phillip Burton introduced legislation for the creation of Golden Gate National Recreation Area, including Olema Valley. The following year this bill passed. The result is a green belt of public land which stretches almost without a break from the tip of Tomales Point to the Golden Gate Bridge. Burton was also responsible for more than doubling the wilderness area of all National Parks and in 1985, the wilderness area of Point Reyes was dedicated to him in recognition of his accomplishments.

While many battles have been won, conservation groups are still very active protecting the wild life and environment of West Marin. Descriptions of the various associations and how to contact them, can be found in the Environmental Groups chapter.

DOUGLAS IRIS
Chimney Rock

LOOKING NORTH TOWARDS TOMALES POINT
from McClure's Beach Outcropping

TIDAL PATTERNS
Drakes Estero near Home Ranch

TREES ON INVERNESS RIDGE BEFORE THE MOUNT VISION FIRE
Inverness Ridge Trail

WAVE AT ELEPHANT ROCK
South of McClure's Beach

DUSK AT LIMANTOUR BEACH

COASTAL HILLS IN MORNING FOG
from Inverness Ridge

GROSSI POND
Pierce Point Road

SOUTH FROM
LIMANTOUR BEACH
AT DUSK

North From
Limantour Beach
at Sunset

COW IN THE FOG
Near the Coast Guard Radio Station

TULE REEDS
Limantour Marsh

GREAT BEACH & THE LIGHT
From the road to Pierce Point

HAWK

POINT REYES HEADLANDS
From Mount Vision

MULTI-COLORED STARFISH
K.P. GOODWIN

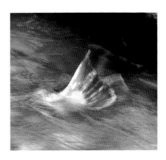

ELK

Emerging from the swirling fog, the herd of tule elk makes a primeval tableau as they slowly forage along the cliffs at the northern end of Point Reyes National Seashore. The elk are impressive animals with magnificent antlers and heavy winter coats.

The sight must have been commonplace to the Coast Miwok people who lived on the Point Reyes peninsula before it was colonized by European settlers.

Reports from Sir Francis Drake mention thousands of very large deer wandering inland from the coast. The combination of hunting and the loss of the native vegetation to agriculture and livestock led to the gradual extinction of tule elk at Point Reyes in the late 1850's.

Adult tule elk were reintroduced to Tomales Point in 1978. The original 13 elk (2 males and 11 females) have now grown to more than 500. There is an ongoing program to reduce their population growth through contraception of the cows.

Summer is rutting season. The males grow huge antlers, 4 feet wide and up to 5 feet high. A set of antlers can weigh up to 40 pounds. Sometimes two young males will spar, antlers interlocked, for the right to take over a harem. Usually only the male leader will impregnate the females though occasionally a young aggressive buck will take his chances. The calves are born in the spring. They nurse for four or five months but start nibbling on grass when less than one month old. Cows which can calve annually, give birth to one calf at a time. Elk are renowned as one of the most polygamous mammals in the world with one male having a large harem.

Park policy is to extend the range of the elk in the park. Twenty seven elk have been transferred to the Limantour Wilderness Area. The Mount Vision fire cleared excessive brush, making it suitable habitat for these magnificent animals.

MOUNTAIN LION
...Felis concolor azteca

The first recorded photograph of a mountain lion in Marin County was taken by a automated camera set up after the Mount Vision fire. Over a period of 3 days, 12 pictures of a mountain lion at night were taken 1/2 mile north of the Bear Valley Trail. Images of the same mountain lion were also recorded near Point Reyes Hill. The camera takes a picture when a beam of light is interrupted. The lion here was photographed at 5:39 pm on August 30, 1998 in the wilderness area. The camera was set up by Scott Berendt, a biologist technician who works with research biologist, Gary Fellers from the Biological Resources Division of the US Geological Survey.

Several people, including myself, have heard the eery sound of the mountain lion on the Inverness Ridge. Unlike the roar of an African lion, the mountain lion sounds more like the scream of a woman. There have been no attacks on people in this park.

About half of California is prime mountain lion country. This simple fact is a surprise to many. These large, powerful predators have always lived here, preying on deer and other wildlife, and playing an important role in the ecosystem. The status of the mountain lion in California evolved from 'bountied predator' between 1907 and 1963, meaning monetary incentives were offered for every mountain lion killed, to 'special protected mammal' in 1990. The change in legal status reflects growing public appreciation and concern for mountain lions.

Like any wildlife, mountain lions can be dangerous. With a better understanding of mountain lions and their habitat, we can coexist with these magnificent animals

ANATOMY: Strong jaws and teeth adapted to seize and kill. Can drag prey up to its own size to secluded spots to eat later. Though most cats' eyes contract to a slit, the mountain lion's eyes remain round. Their legs are strong, which allows them the speed to kill quickly.

SENSES: Excellent binocular vision for judging distance to its prey.

Photograph of lion by Scott Berendt & Gary Fellers.   41

LOCOMOTION: Lions have tremendous leaping power, because the hind legs are longer than the forelegs. They can leap 18 feet in one jump. The tail is used for balance. They walk on their toes, rather than their soles and are silent runners because of retractable claws. They stalk prey.

ACTIVITY PERIOD: Nocturnal; normally hunting at night, but may be forced to hunt during the day if prey is scarce.

SOCIAL UNIT: Solitary except for breeding and when the female is raising cubs.

REPRODUCTION: Females breed at 3 years of age. There is no definite breeding season; 3-4 cubs are born after 90-96 days. Cubs are weaned at 3 months.

PHYSICAL APPEARANCE: The mountain lion is tawny-colored with black-tipped ears and tail. Although smaller than the jaguar, it is one of North America's largest cats. Adult males may be more than 8 feet long, from nose to end of tail, and generally weigh between 130 and 150 pounds. Adult females can be 7 feet long and weigh between 65 and 90 pounds. Mountain lion kittens, or cubs, are covered with blackish-brown spots and have dark rings around their tails. The markings fade as they mature.

Mountain lions are very powerful carnivores and normally prey upon deer, elk, and large animals. However, they can survive preying on small animals as well. They usually hunt alone, at night. They prefer to ambush their prey, often from behind. They usually kill with a powerful bite below the base of the skull, breaking the neck. They often cover the carcass with dirt,or leaves and may come back to feed on it over the course of a few days. Their generally secretive and solitary nature is what makes it possible for humans to live in mountain lion country without ever seeing a mountain lion.

An adult male's home range often spans over 100 square miles. Females generally use smaller areas--about twenty to sixty square miles.

In California, mountain lion populations have grown. In 1920, a rough estimate put their number at 600. Since then, more accurate estimates, based on field studies, revealed a population of more than 2,000 mountain lions in the 1970's. Today's estimate ranges between 4,000-6,000.

A mountain lion's natural life span is probably about 12 years in the wild and up to 25 years in captivity. Natural enemies include other large predators such as bears, lions and, at one time in California, wolves. They also fall victim to accidents, disease, road hazards and people. Generally, mountain lions are calm, quiet and elusive. They are most commonly found in areas with plentiful prey and adequate cover. Such conditions exist in West Marin. Consequently, the number of mountain lion / human interactions has increased. Even so, the potential for being killed or injured by a mountain lion is quite low compared to many other natural hazards. There is a far greater risk, for example, of being struck by lightning than of being attacked by a mountain lion.

WHAT SHOULD YOU DO IF YOU ENCOUNTER A MOUNTAIN LION?

There's been very little research on how to avoid mountain lion attacks. But mountain lion attacks that have occurred are being analyzed in the hope that some crucial questions can be answered: Did the victim do something to inadvertently provoke an attack? What should a person who is approached by a mountain lion do--or not do? The following suggestions are based on studies of mountain lion behavior and analysis of attacks by mountain lions, tigers and leopards:

DO NOT HIKE ALONE: Go in groups, with adults supervising children.

KEEP CHILDREN CLOSE TO YOU: Observations of captured wild mountain lions reveal that the animals seem especially drawn to children. Keep children within your sight at all times.

DO NOT APPROACH A LION: Most mountain lions will try to avoid a confrontation. Give them a way to escape.

DO NOT RUN FROM A LION: Running may stimulate a mountain lion's instinct to chase. Instead, stand and face the animal. Make eye contact. If you have small children with you, pick them up if possible so they don't panic and run. Although it may be awkward, pick them up without bending over or turning away from the mountain lion.

DO NOT CROUCH DOWN OR BEND OVER: In Nepal, a researcher studying tigers and leopards watched the big cats kill cattle and domestic water buffalo while ignoring humans standing nearby. He surmised that a human standing up is just not the right shape for a cat's prey. On the other hand, a person squatting or bending over looks a lot like a four-legged prey animal. If you're in mountain lion country, avoid squatting, crouching or bending over, even when picking up children.

DO ALL YOU CAN TO APPEAR LARGER: Raise your arms. Open your jacket if you are wearing one. Again, pick up small children. Throw stones, branches, or whatever you can reach without crouching or turning your back. Wave your arms slowly and speak firmly in a loud voice. The idea is to convince the mountain lion that you are not prey and that you may be a danger to it.

FIGHT BACK IF ATTACKED: A hiker in Southern California used a rock to fend off a mountain lion that was attacking his son. Others have fought back successfully with sticks, caps, jackets, garden tools and their bare hands. Since a mountain lion usually tries to bite the head or neck, try to remain standing and face the attacking animal.

In an innovative program, Point Reyes National Seashore scientists are collecting data on the populations of reptiles, amphibians and animals in the park. The basic survey unit is a y-shaped array, about 100 feet across, comprising buckets, wire mesh cylinders, aluminum boxes and wooden boards which, in various ways, trap animals without injuring them. Eight sites in the park each have four arrays and a camera that automatically takes a picture when a light beam is interrupted. This is how the mountain lion picture was obtained. By having the same series of arrays at different locations, researchers can compare animal populations. With information collected over many years it is possible to obtain accurate data on the status of a large area. Thus park managers can base conservation efforts on real facts.

GREAT BLUE HERON

EGRETS AND HERONS

Picking their way along the edges of Tomales Bay, the elegant long legged great blue heron and great egret are a dramatic and not too rare sight in West Marin. Their major nesting site in the area is Audubon Canyon Ranch, on Bolinas Lagoon. These birds will travel up to 22 kms to forage so their feeding grounds include Tomales Bay, the Limantour estuary and Nicasio Reservoir.

Walking down to Limantour Beach one day, I stopped to watch a great blue heron wading in the wetlands beside the path. Suddenly the heron darted towards the water. It straightened itself and in its beak dangled a small snake. It hung precariously for a while and then became the heron's next meal. I could see the slow progress of the snake winding down the heron's long neck. It was a remarkable achievement.

The breeding cycle of great blue herons and great egrets can be broken roughly into four week segments. Eggs are incubated for four weeks. The young chicks are guarded or brooded, by either parent, for four weeks. The chicks, then quite voracious, can protect themselves fairly well against marauding ravens and other predators so both parents are free to go out and forage. After a further four weeks the nestlings begin to fly and four weeks later they are independent. The parents fly off while the young generally stay in the nesting area for a while until perhaps they realize their parents are not going to come back and then they too fly away.

EGRET FISHING AT SUNSET

PELICAN DIVING
Drakes Bay with Chimney Rock in background

PELICANS

Long single lines of low flying brown pelican skimming the waves are a wonderful sight in May when they return to Point Reyes after breeding in mid winter on the Channel Islands and offshore islands in the Sea of Cortez. The American white pelican which breed on islands on landlocked lakes of the North American West, head to Point Reyes in August usually staying here until January.

Brown and white pelican have distinctive hunting styles. The brown pelican hunts independently, catching fish by "dive bombing" their victims. White pelican work as a group in the shallow waters of a bay, lake or estuary. They surround a school of fish until it is concentrated into a small area and then scoop up their prey in their huge bills.

Both species of pelican were badly affected by DDT. The Californian population of brown pelican declined by 90 percent and it was classified as endangered. Since DDT was banned in this country, the numbers of both species have rebounded.

ADULT BROWN PELICAN
In breeding plumage

NATIVE DEER AND DOC OTTINGER'S EXOTICS

An excursion to the Point Reyes National Seashore almost guarantees the sighting of deer. Native to the area is the black tailed or "mule" deer. In the 1940's and 50's Doc Ottinger imported axis and fallow deer for hunting.

The axis deer comes from India while the fallow deer is indigenous to the Mediterranean region of Europe and Asia Minor. Most of the imported fallow deer were pure white so they would be easy to hunt. However these deer also are brown, black and mixed. Both exotics are commonly seen near Bear Valley, sometimes even in the same herd, though there is no evidence of interbreeding.

KGB

ELEPHANT SEALS

After an absence of more than 150 years, the Northern elephant seals have returned to the shores of Point Reyes in increasing numbers since 1981. They have established colonies at the northern end of Drakes Beach and on the shores below the Point Reyes Headlands.

Elephant seals are prodigious long distance swimmers. The males make the journey from Alaska to California twice a year. Bulls, females and weaners (or juveniles) travel independently. The cows give birth at Point Reyes during winter after a gestation period of 9 to 10 months. Pups are weaned after a month and the cows leave for the open ocean. The pups stay a month longer and then they too go to sea. They and the cows return at the end of spring to molt and then go back to sea to eat. The bulls meanwhile leave in March, travel to Alaska and return in June and July to molt.

The elephant seals all return to the Pacific coast in the late fall and winter to begin the cycle once more. Not much is known of their eating habits as they dive up to a mile deep for their food. They can stay under water for almost two hours. They rely on a thick layer of subcutaneous fat for insulation and use this fat for energy when fasting onshore for long periods. It was this fat that almost caused them to be hunted to extinction in the 1800's. A bull elephant seal could yield nearly 25 gallons of heating oil.

Richard and I were escorted by Ranger Dawn Adams, to photograph the elephant seals as great care has to be taken when approaching a colony to avoid disturbing them. The males can weigh up to 5,000 pounds and reach 16 feet in length. The male proboscis or snout is used to trumpet. The alpha male usually makes the deepest sounds. Perhaps even more impressive than their physical presence was the harmony of sounds the colony made - high notes of the pups, usually mellow tones of the females and then the bass of the males. The alpha male trumpets to warn off other males who might be moving in on his harem. If a male is approaching a cow, she will make a noise indicating whether she is receptive to mating. Sometimes a young male with a small proboscis will sneak in among the females and try and copulate. An alpha male remains the king pin for 1 to 2 years. The bulls reach their peak at 9 years and generally live about 15 years. The females begin breeding at 3 to 4 years old. They usually live longer than the bulls. The oldest known age of a female at Point Reyes Headlands was 21 years.

This information was provided by the Senior Science Advisor at Point Reyes National Seashore, Dr. Sarah Allen.

SPOTTED OWL
Near Indian Beach, Tomales Bay State Park
Endangered by clearcutting old growth forests

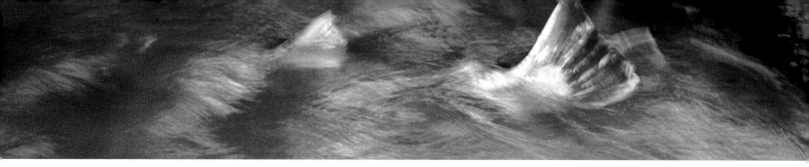

THE COHO SALMON RUN

Our house sitting saga is perhaps hard to beat. We advertised in the local newspaper, the Point Reyes Light for a house to rent or housesit while we were rebuilding our house after the Mount Vision fire. We were offered a 30 room farm house in Woodacre which had been built in 1903. It was on the market and needed a caretaker. San Geronimo Creek runs across one end of the property and we were very happy to oblige.

One morning we saw some people standing on "our bridge". We thought they were teenagers and prepared to give them the big lecture. On closer inspection (the driveway is rather long) we realized they were "responsible adults" who when I said they would need to see the house with a realtor, replied they were looking at the salmon. There were indeed five salmon swimming up the creek. They had made their way up a stream which at times is only a couple of feet wide, in other places just a few inches deep. They used their tails to move themselves up the shallow parts seeking a predetermined destination.

Scientists think the chemistry of the stream is implanted in the coho at birth. As adult fish, they swim in the ocean and can detect the taste of the fresh water streams merging with the seawater. When they are three years old, they know they need to return to their particular stream to spawn. Their taste is not infallible, some salmon will choose a different stream or tributary particularly if the water is turgid. Despite what I learned from the scientists I could not help think that perhaps the salmon were choosing the small streams for spawning as they knew they would give their young a safe sanctuary.

We watched the coho for hours. Occasionally there was great activity as four or five salmon swam up and over each other, splashing and jostling, the males trying to keep others away from their chosen female. Females lay between 2500 and 3000 eggs. They do not put "all their eggs in one basket", choosing instead to build several nests, or redds, by swimming on their side and digging a trench in the sand. The eggs will be fertilized almost immediately by a male who discharges millions of spawn or milt over the eggs. Sometimes the eggs are fertilized by different males. There is usually a 98% success rate for fertilization.

It takes about 50 days for a coho egg to hatch in a stream whose temperature is 50 degrees fahrenheit, less time if the water is warmer. It lives in the stream for a year, and then when it is four or five inches long, it swims to the ocean.

The coho lead short perilous lives. The streams may dry up leaving them either stranded or prey to birds; they can be eaten by seals or sea lions or caught by fishermen; although they usually keep to the western side of the Pacific, they have been known to swim to the Asiatic coast and back in their two year sojourn in the sea. As the females enter their chosen stream, the different chemistry of fresh water starts the maturing process of the eggs. The female then races against her biological clock to reach the place where she wants to lay her eggs.

Even in the hatcheries, only half a percent of the fertilized eggs reach maturity. The coho give their all for their young. Days after spawning, both male and female die. The amount of time they have to enjoy their place of birth depends on the distance upstream they have swum. In West Marin where they swim about 25 miles upstream, they might live five days after spawning. In areas where they have traveled 100 miles in fresh water to spawn, they will have exhausted all their reserves and will survive only a few hours. We saw a vulture take a dead salmon out of the water. It did not take the natural world long to recycle.

If there are heavy rains after the spawning, there is a danger that the movement of silt will smother the eggs which have to be constantly breathing in oxygen. More rarely, heavy flooding can wash away the stream bed and its redds.

Coho have been declared a threatened species from Fort Bragg to Santa Cruz. This requires that the Federal Government oversee a restoration program of the habitat of the coho. As the logging companies are responsible for most of the silt in the streams, the classification of the coho as threatened, has wide reaching repercussions.

THE GREAT BEACH
North from the Point Reyes Lighthouse

THE FARALLON ISLANDS
From Inverness Ridge

SEA PALMS
Kehoe Beach

CLIFFS AT DRAKES BAY

Like the painting *Icarus Falling into the Sea*, where a tiny leg sticking out of the water is all one sees of Icarus, this whale sighting of a Humpback blowing does not show too much whale. Whales can be just dots on the horizon, but even when a whale is observed from afar, people feel good inside. Maybe those big whale brains are communicating their joy of being alive. – R.P.B.

WHALE MIGRATION

The most common whale seen in West Marin is the Gray Whale. Starting in November, they migrate from Alaska down to the warm waters of Baja. The whales both mate and give birth in the warm, shallow Scammon's Lagoon and Magdalena Bay on Baja's Pacific coast. After several months, when the newborn calves are ready to swim north, the whales leave in small groups. Alaska is their summer habitat where the sea

WHALE AT MAGDALENA BAY

provides them with the most food.

The best place to watch the migration is at the Point Reyes Lighthouse jutting into the Pacific Ocean. However, sometimes one can be fortunate elsewhere. Richard and I were bicycling along the trail from Coast Camp when we spotted four Gray Whales swimming northward just fifty feet offshore! From our elevated position on the cliff we had a perfect view of two females with their calves. They were so close we could see barnacles on their huge bodies. They swam in circles for a while as if playing in the water, now and then lifting their heads and opening their mouths, so we could see water streaming through their baleen. They slowly made their way up the coast while we followed on our bicycles along the path at the edge of the cliff. They entranced us for 30 minutes (naturally we did not have cameras with us) and then headed to deeper waters.

Other species of whales, though more rare, are seen off the shores of West Marin. Sightings of Humpbacks, once seriously endangered, have become more common.

A huge Mitsubishi salt evaporation project is now proposed for Magdalena Bay.

LIMANTOUR SAND SPIT AND THE SOUTHERN COAST
Aerial view

ERODED CLIFFS AT SUNSET
Sculptured Beach

WAVE AND CHIMNEY ROCK
Drakes Beach

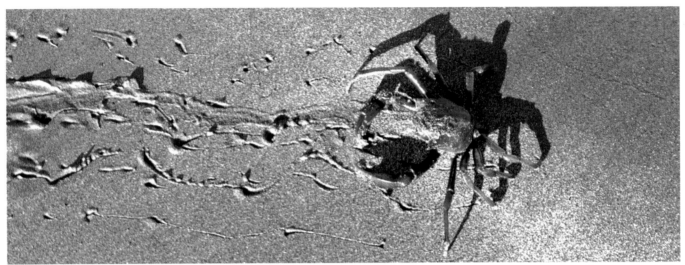

CRAB MUSICAL SCORE
Sculpted Beach

DRAKES BAY CLEARING STORM
From Chimney Rock looking towards Mount Helena

BREAKING WAVES AT DUSK
Limantour Beach

OCEAN AND BOLINAS LAGOON AT DUSK
Above Stinson Beach from Mt. Tamalpais

TOMALES BAY BEACHES

Tomales Bay is 13 miles long, one mile wide, and generally quite shallow with wide expanses of mud flats exposed at low tide. Consequently over the summer months the water in the bay reaches an easily tolerable temperature. Teachers Beach, also known as Chicken Ranch Beach, just beyond Inverness, is the most accessible beach. However the bottom of the bay at that point is covered with small rocks and one is well advised to don some footwear before venturing in. Shell Beach (one and two) further down the shore requires a hike through a beautiful forest to reach the beach. A swimming raft between the two coves makes a challenging destination. Lying on the raft and warming up in the sun after a swim is a wonderful pleasure life sometimes offers.

Heart's Desire Beach, approached from the road to Pierce Point, is the most popular beach on Tomales Bay. It is part of Tomales Bay State Park. There are picnic tables on bluffs with spectacular views overlooking the bay. A short hike north of Heart's Desire leads to Indian Beach which has replicas of three Coast Miwok buildings on the shore. Built of redwood bark, they have the same shape as teepees but should last about 60 years.

The entrance of Tomales Bay is renowned as a breeding ground for the great white shark. There have been no recorded shark attacks within Tomales Bay though skindivers diving for abalone near Tomales Point have had encounters with sharks. The greater danger is entering or leaving the bay by boat at the the wrong time. Numerous people have drowned when their boats have been sunk by sneaker waves which form at the sand bar at the mouth of Tomales Bay. Shallow water causes the waves to break. Experienced sailors know to time their departures and arrivals at slack high tide to secure a safe passage when the ocean swell and winds are low.

DRAKES BEACH

Protected by the Point Reyes Headlands, Drakes Beach usually has gentle surf. Sometimes the coast will be shrouded in fog, yet this the beach will have sunshine. Whales, particularly mothers with their calves, quite often swim into the bay on their migration up the coast.

Sir Francisco Drakes is reputed to have landed at Drakes Bay and exclaimed that the cliffs reminded him of the "White cliffs of Dover". Pottery dating to 1579, the year Drake landed on the west coast, has been found on this beach.

A path north of the parking lot, leads up to the spectacular Peter Behr Overlook, named after the man who played a big part in preserving this area as a national park. A rare treat at this beach is the oyster burgers and other great food served at the Drakes Beach Cafe. It's real home cooking in a national park. The chefs, Jonne Le Meiux and Gloria Padilla, are locals and use seafood caught locally.

LIMANTOUR BEACH

Sand castle competitions are a staple of West Marin life

Limantour Beach offers constant surprises. In winter, hundreds of redwing blackbirds roost in the wetlands that parallel the beach. At dusk they wheel and turn in huge flocks, looking like musical notes swirling through the air, dividing into different scores of perfect harmony. I have seen whales frolicking offshore and have been accompanied by seals swimming along the shoreline while I walked on the beach.

Further north, the entrance to the Limantour Estero is a favorite haulout site of harbor seals. Sometimes one will see perhaps twenty seals of all ages basking on the beach just above the tide line. They are easily disturbed so to enjoy the sight, sit on the beach some distance away and watch them through binoculars.

Since the Mount Vision fire of 1995, the lupine near the beach has grown more vigorously than ever before and is very colorful in the spring. The fragrance of the lupine is intoxicating. Rodents who escaped the fire are more exposed in the new growth so the number of Northern Harriers hunting nearby has risen considerably.

THE GREAT BEACH INCLUDING NORTH AND SOUTH BEACHES

North of the Point Reyes lighthouse, the Great Beach extends eleven miles. The ocean is wild and the currents strong. One day Richard found a bottle containing a note lying on the sand at the high tide mark. It was dated just a week earlier and said that the bottle had been dropped into the Russian River at Guerneville as a school science project. We were amazed it had traveled so quickly. It shows how fast pollution from another area can travel with ocean currents down the coast.

The beaches on this side of the Point Reyes headlands offer very good beachcombing. Another time we found an electric light bulb made in Poland and despite its long sojourn in the ocean it still worked! I guess it wasn't screwed in well.

ABBOTTS LAGOON, KEHOE BEACH AND MCCLURES BEACH

Kehoe Beach is an interesting beach because of its granite cliffs and rock formations. It is like seeing a section of Death Valley at the ocean. A great hike is a loop south from Kehoe Beach to Abbotts Lagoon or even North or South Beaches alongside the ocean. One returns by hitching a ride on the Pierce Point road or leaving a car at both ends. At the end of Pierce Point Road is the short trail to McClure's Beach. On the southern part of the beach is a dramatic rock pushing its way out to sea. From its peak are spectacular views of the coast line. A little further out to sea is a small rocky island, a favorite perch of pelicans, cormorants and seagulls.

POND SWIMMING

FRESH WATER SWIMMING IS AVAILABLE at various dams and lakes throughout the park. One skinny dipping haven is Hagmaier's Pond near Five Brooks Trailhead. I witnessed a sight there straight from a movie set. It was a beautiful day and a couple of dozen people were enjoying the sun when over the hill came a naked woman, with long hair, riding a beautiful horse. She rode into the dam, jumped off the horse's back and they both swam in the water. Five minutes later she climbed back on the horse, rode out of the dam and disappeared like a mirage over the hill.

SURFING IN WEST MARIN

UNTIL RECENTLY, swimming or surfing was illegal at the sometimes extremely rough beaches north of the lighthouse. However after a prolonged battle, with surfers being arrested and fined, the law was changed and people can now enter the water at their own risk. Drakes Beach offers the safest surfing, both body and board in West Marin. Fishing seems to be more dangerous with people being swept off rocks or pulled into heavy surf every season.

SURFER & FISHING BOAT AT DUSK
Entrance, Bolinas Lagoon

It was my birthday at the end of October, a warm Indian summer day, and we were walking along Stinson Beach. I watched the surfers enviously as they took the waves. Suddenly I thought, "It's my birthday and I can do what I want!" Off I ran to the surf shop and rented a wet suit and boogie board. My first wave was a dream. I caught it from the beginning and surfed ecstatically all the way to the shore. I surfed for an hour, until my feet were blue. It was one of my best birthdays.

Stinson Beach is not always so benevolent. Swimmers need to keep a wary eye on the currents. One particular wave wrenched my board out of my hands. I was surprised at how difficult it was to get back to shore. Another danger is sharks. We recently had our first shark attack at Stinson Beach. A 16 year old boy, Jonathan Kathrein, was bitten by a great white shark while boogy boarding fifty yards off shore. He managed to fight off the shark by grabbing its gills. It let go of Jonathan's leg and he swam to shore. He is expected to recover fully though he has 200 stitches in his right thigh. Statistically, it's more dangerous driving to the beach than swimming in a shark habitat, but the fear of being eaten is hard to overcome!

AUTHOR'S FOOTPRINT

PHOTOGRAPHER'S REFLECTION

LIGHTHOUSES OF THE WEST MARIN COAST

ABOVE THE POINT REYES LIGHTHOUSE

POINT REYES LIGHTHOUSE AT DUSK

LIGHTHOUSES

POINT REYES is the foggiest point on the Pacific coast. It is also the nation's windiest headland, with north westerlies sometimes blowing over 130 miles per hour! The first recorded shipwreck off its shores was the San Augustin which broke up and landed at Drake's Beach in 1595.

As a result of this shipwreck, for years it was impossible to tell whether 16th century artifacts found on the beach came from this wreck or the Golden Hind, captained by Sir Francis Drake, which had careened on the west coast in 1579. However, new historical evidence has revealed that the pattern on the china washed up on Drakes Beach dated from the late 1570's and apparently the pattern on fashionable china changed almost every year.

The fog hid the coastline and granite rocks from many ship captains. After more than 60 shipwrecks in the area, the Point Reyes lighthouse was built in 1870. It was forged from iron plate and bolted into solid rock in the cliff. This lighthouse was notorious as a desolate place to work. The job was extremely arduous and morale was often low. The lighthouse is reached by walking down 308 steep stairs. When it was first built, the manually operated fog horn was housed in a building 638 steps further down the cliff.

The lantern room contains a fresnel lens, 7'10" high, which weighs three tons. Manufactured in Paris, it was ingeniously designed so that the thousand hand ground prisms in the lens could focus the weak light of oil lamps into 24 powerful rays. These rays could be seen up to 30 miles out to sea.

The first order fresnel lens, so called because it is the largest lens of its type, is no longer operational on a daily basis. Occasionally it is switched on for public viewing and one sees the lens itself slowly turning.

The lighthouse was automated in 1975 with the installation of an automated reflecting light, electric fog signal and radio beacon equipment. The National Park Service took control of the lighthouse which is now open to the public. It is an excellent location for whale-watching in the winter.

POINT REYES LIGHTHOUSE STEPS

THE POINT REYES LIGHTHOUSE
From the steps

When a ship loses her way and is swept on to the rocks, the power of the sea makes short work of her destruc-
tion. Few survive the icy water and the pounding of the surf. Lighthouses are vital to save lives, even in this era
of satellite navigation.

The early crews of the lifesaving stations on the coast had this grim motto;

"You have to go out; but you don't have to come back."

THE POINT BONITA LIGHTHOUSE

WEATHER IN WEST MARIN

Weather here is unusual. This area has one of the least variations in temperature between the summer and winter in the United States. The average temperature (day and night) in winter is 50 degrees fahrenheit, only five degrees colder than the summer average of 55 degrees. We have a long and intense rainy season in winter but people are surprised that our summer is foggy and cold as well. Spring has clear weather with strong winds from the northwest. Our fall is an Indian summer, with hot, sunny days which warm up Tomales Bay to swimmable temperatures. The climate is tempered by the ocean and the North Pacific High, a mass of cool air 1000 miles off the California coast which deflects rain storms away in the summer. When the Pacific High decreases in magnitude towards the end of summer, the rain starts in November. Winter rains and wind can hit West Marin with ferocity while the summer fog occasionally settles in for weeks. More often the fog burns off mid-morning and returns in the late afternoon. The cycle produces mysterious landscapes with fingers of fog drifting through canyons. Sometimes at sunset, fog will cover the coastal mountains, a band of sky will be crimson and above, high clouds will glow yellow and orange.

When fog blows by trees, particularly Bishop Pines, water will condense on the needles and drip to the ground thus providing water for the forest. Putting a container under a "dripper" produced half an inch a day of fresh water!

MAILBOXES IN PAPERMILL CREEK
White House Pool

FLOODED LEVEE ROAD (SIR FRANCIS DRAKE)

INDIAN SUMMER IN THE FOREST
Inverness Ridge

One year the shores of Tomales Bay froze for a week. Occasionally snow falls on Inverness ridge and local mountain tops but it generally melts within a few hours. The lower portion of Tomales Bay regularly floods over the levee blocking roads and access to emergency services. The community is renowned for pulling together in time of crisis. We prepare for winter with candles, a closet of Goretex rain jackets and stockpiles of food. The power often goes out for up to three days after a big storm when trees, blown over by winter winds, fall on the power lines. Winds at the lighthouse are clocked at hurricane force. Since the Mt. Vision fire there is no wind break from the trees, which died. We wonder if our windows will hold as they flex, assaulted by water driven at fire nozzle intensity by the wind. We love the views but fear the winter storms.

SUNSET AND FOG
Inverness Ridge

DAWN, OLEMA VALLEY AND BOLINAS RIDGE
Inverness Ridge

MOUNT VISION FIRE AT 7:00 PM FROM HIGHWAY ONE
Northern Point Reyes Station

FIRE AT 2:00 PM FROM HIGHWAY ONE

BOMBER DROPS RETARDANT

THE MOUNT VISION FIRE

On October 1, 1995 four boys went camping at a secret campground on the slopes of Mount Vision. Before they left the camp site, they threw water on

KATHLEEN AT THE CABIN
Inverness Park

their camp fire and then covered it with sand. They thought they had been responsible campers. The next day, hot dry winds fanned the still smoldering ashes which burst into flames.

Three miles away, Richard and I were in our cabin on the top of Inverness Ridge. We had just returned from Bali the previous night and now, looking afresh at our land covered with huckleberry, ferns and a thick forest of trees, we told ourselves how fortunate we were to live in such a place. We decided to cut down a dead tree. A friend, Scott Patterson, a volunteer for the Inverness Fire Department, stopped to give a hand. While we were talking he was paged. A vegetation fire had started on Mount Vision. It was 1:30 PM. He rushed off.

Within ten minutes we could see blue smoke in the valley below our cabin. We had a bad feeling about the direction of the wind and told our neighbor our misgivings. We decided to drive to the eastern side of Tomales Bay so we could observe and photograph the fire's progress.

We drove up Highway One, north of Point Reyes Station, and parked at a pull out directly across Tomales Bay from the brush fire. We saw a helicopter drop water, which it had picked up in a bucket from

HELICOPTER
Millerton Point

the bay, on the fire. After a few runs the helicopter had to refuel. An aerial bomber dropped fire retardant but shortly afterwards the fierce winds blew burning embers across the vegetation choked upper canyon. Spot fires erupted in two locations in the next valley which were much more difficult for the firefighters to attack. The combination of low humidity, high winds and a tinder dry forest thick with undergrowth, soon made the conflagration unstoppable.

We watched in horror as the fire grew in intensity. Bishop pine trees, full of flammable oils and resins, exploded into flames as the fire spread through the tops of the trees. The sun turned red as the smoke increased. More helicopters and airplanes arrived to help. Finally we realized that the fire was definitely heading in the direction of our cabin and was completely out of control. We called neighbors on our cell phone warning them of the possibility of impending disaster, then jumped into our car to go back to the

THE LAND BEFORE THE FIRE

cabin to retrieve some valuables. Our cabin is 11/2 miles up a narrow winding road. The road was strangely deserted as the area was evacuated.

The light on the trees and bushes on our property was eerily orange. The smell of smoke was overwhelming, but we could not see the fire in progress. We had no idea how much time we had and ran up and down our hill trying to pack the car. We took paintings, bicycles, personal treasures. I had a large painting in the cabin but, in the anxiety of the moment, did not think to cut it off its stretcher bars and roll it up. We drove down Drakes View Drive, passing seven fire engines going in the opposite direction. There was a roadblock at the bottom of the road. Our timing was perfect.

We headed back across Tomales Bay for a front row seat. It was a schizophrenic experience to watch Inverness Ridge burn. We knew hundreds of lives were in danger, our neighborhood was in flames, yet it was an awesomely beautiful sight.

THE FIRE AT 6:30 PM

The moon was almost full, the ridge was black, the trees outlined in orange and red, huge billowing clouds of white and gray rising above the ridge line. Behind them, the sky was deep blue and the fire reflected red in the water of Tomales Bay.

The fire had at first been contained to 21/2 acres. Winds of 50 mph caused the first fatal jump. From that moment, it became extremely difficult to fight. Over 2,100 people from 100 agencies all over California were brought in to fight the blaze. Forty eight homes were destroyed and over 12,000 acres of Point Reyes National Seashore (about 17 percent of the park) were burned. Fortunately the fire traveled, down to the Pacific Ocean rather than into Inverness. The wind never permanently changed direction towards Tomales Bay, thus saving many more homes. There were only 12 minor injuries and many pets were saved.

Living on the top of Inverness Ridge was like living with a time bomb. There had not been a serious fire there for more than 60 years. The bomb went off and lives were shattered. Perhaps it will grow more beautiful as the Bishop Pine, which only seed through fire, regenerate. The ferns and huckleberry will

SMOKE AND SUN APPARITION
I see an image of a giant flying creature with the sun for a heart and the blue sky defining its wings. –R.B.

BURNING BISHOP PINE STUMP
Inverness Ridge

Tree stumps burned for several days.
We found holes in the ground 4 feet
deep where the roots were burning.
These fire-holes were very dangerous.

CABIN SITE AFTER FIRE
Inverness Ridge

All traces of vegetation were gone and the ground was covered with ash. The white area in the middle background was our cabin, reduced to powder and molten glass and metal.

start growing again in the spring. The ridge should be a safer place to live now. Those houses which were not affected will clear around their homes, and much of the park is cleared of dead trees and brush, allowing new growth.

We sifted though the remains of our cabin and found a pair of metal candle sticks, still intact, which Richard's grandfather brought from Russia in the early 1900's. With a group of friends and volunteers, we shoveled ashes in to garbage bags. Two trips to the dump, and the cabin became a memory. Soon there will be no sign it was ever there.

Having recently returned from Bali, maybe we have a different philosophical perspective. In Bali, we had witnessed and photographed many cremations. They seemed a natural part of life. In that culture, cremations are a public event, a celebration of the person's life and a freeing of the soul.

As artists, Richard and I found the only way to deal with the situation, given that we are not trained firefighters, was to record it with our cameras and our writing. We made images of the fire to remember what happened, to analyze it later, to capture the beauty of this phoenix–like transformation from old to young forest. The great cycle of life rolls on and we should not hurry or retard this process, an essential to the life of the ecosystem we are a part of.

At the coast near Limantour Beach it is easy to forget the fire ever happened. The first spring brought spectacular luminous green growth. All the old dead vegetation had been removed by the fire. The seeds in the soil exploded with life as they did not have to compete with older growth. The wildflowers, grasses and shrubs returned more abundant than ever.

On Inverness Ridge the huckleberry bushes and ferns came back as expected and miniature forests of bishop pine appeared all over ridge. Invasive weeds like thistle took advantage of the cleared vegetation to make a strong stand but so too did the wildflowers, which were more visible than before. That first spring, lupine covered whole hillsides with blue sweetly smelling blossoms. Panoramic views to the ocean were revealed as thousands of dead trees lost their needles.

The fire burned so hot that few trees lived. On our land, three trees survived. However shoots have sprouted from some of the tree roots.

Many of the people who lost their homes have rebuilt. Neighbors have grown closer as they share their experiences and frustrations in the building process. We flew over the area in a small airplane. Before the fire on a similar flight we could not find our land because of the dense foliage, now it looked like a barren mountain top.

Surprisingly, there are more birds nesting in the burned land than in unburned adjacent areas. Researchers think that the reason is the reduced number of predators like snakes and woodrats as well as the vigorous growth of the new vegetation Tule elk have

OUR MELTED WINDOW FRAME

LUPINE AFTER FIRE
Inverness Ridge trail

been introduced north of Limantour Road, a section of the park which was burned in the fire and cleared of dense undergrowth. This could help solve the problem of overpopulation at Tomales Point where the 13 original elk reintroduced to the area in 1978 has grown to over 500.

A mountain lion has been photographed on Mount Vision on a research camera set up by the park service to record animal life returning to the area. Also photographed was the rare Point Reyes mountain beaver which people feared had not survived the conflagration.

TOMALES BAY

Lying sheltered from the Pacific Ocean by Inverness Ridge, Tomales Bay is a pristine inland sea with water so pure that even the sensitive oyster can flourish in it. Shrouded in mist with branches overhanging its shores, it has a mysterious beauty.

Often, its glassy surface is a refuge from wild surf. At low tide it is possible to walk for miles along the shore. On a sunny day with children playing on its beaches, it is an innocent playground but if the wind comes up and the fog rolls in, it can provide a challenging experience for all plying its waters.

Thirteen miles long and a mile wide, Tomales Bay is an expression of the San Andreas fault which lies directly beneath it. The fault is a crack in the earth's crust which separates the North American plate and the northward moving Pacific plate. The great San Francisco earthquake of 1906 was centered at the end of the bay.

Tomales Bay is quite shallow with wide expanses of mud flats exposed at low tide. The tidal wetlands near Point Reyes Station were reduced after levees were built on either side of Papermill Creek in 1945 to increase pasture lands. At press time Point Reyes National Seashore had received funding to buy the farmland and restore the wetlands.

The bay supports a large bird population year round and is an important winter feeding ground for 20,000 shorebirds and 25,000 waterfowl. White and brown Pelican favor the bay as a fishing ground. Both Great Egrets and Snowy Egrets are often seen fishing in the shallow waters. It is also a place of refuge for migratory birds. In January 1987 a rare Siberian brown shrike was spotted on the southern end of the bay. Bird watchers came from all over the US to observe this bird.

When the bay is quiet and we are floating offshore, the sound of the wing beats of huge flocks of birds taking off is aching beautiful.

The bay is a major spawning ground of the Pacific herring, second in importance in California only to San Francisco Bay. The herring eggs attach themselves to sub–tidal vegetation, mostly eelgrass. Diving birds, like Surf Scoters and Greater Scaup, snip off eel grass coated with eggs, bring it to the surface and eat the eggs. Over 20 species of birds eat herring eggs. Herring have been fished commercially in Tomales Bay since the 1930's but in order to protect the species, a quota has been in place for the past 23 years. The eelgrass is also home to the bay pipefish which looks like an elongated sea horse.

Coho Salmon and steelhead rainbow trout use streams which flow into Tomales Bay for spawning. Both species were at one time abundant in the Bay. Nowadays they are rare though their numbers are gradually increasing as environmentalists work hard to protect their habitat.

GREAT EGRET

Over the summer months, the water in the bay reaches an easily tolerable temperature for swimming. A swim with a full moon rising behind Elephant Mountain is an adventure not to be missed. If you are very lucky you might even swim alongside a seal.

Congresswoman Lynn Woolsey and MALT are working on a bill which will allow Congress to buy the conservation easements of a continuous strip of farms on the east side of Tomales Bay. Participation in the program will be voluntary for ranchers. The bill will

ELEPHANT MOUNTAIN REFLECTIONS DURING EL NINO
Extreme upper end of Tomales Bay at high tide.
PHOTOGRAPH BY KATHLEEN GOODWIN

help to preserve this side of the bay from development by paying rancher's approximately half the value of their land so they keep it in farming. See the Beach Report (ocean chapter) and the Environmental Groups chapter to learn more about Tomales Bay.

WINDING STREAM IN SALT GRASS
Tomales Bay

MONTEREY STYLE FISHING BOATS
Marshall, California

WEST SHORE IN MIST
Near Children's Beach, Tomales Bay

*Old dock pilings with overhanging
tree limbs on a fade-to-fog morning.*

FJORD STYLE ROWING BOATS
Marshall,California
These wooden boats are based on a old Norwegian design. The high ends are good for riding through the waves and chop on rough days on Tomales Bay.

ELEPHANT MOUNTAIN AND THE MOUTH OF PAPERMILL CREEK
Pasture land to be restored to Tomales Bay wetlands

LICHEN & MOSS
Near Shell Beach, Tomales Bay

MARSH AT INDIAN BEACH
Tomales Bay State Park

AN ARTIST and a fisherman, Clayton Lewis was legendary in West Marin. Nationally recognized for his paintings, jewelry and sculpture, he had a local reputation as a raconteur, sea dog, ladies man and general wit. He died in September of 1995.

Thirty two years before, Clayton was sailing on Tomales Bay with a friend, when he spotted a cove with some intriguing old buildings. He and his friend swam to shore to explore. As soon as he set foot on Laird's Landing, just south of Marshall Beach, Clayton said he knew he had found his home. He contacted the owner of the place and told him the buildings were disintegrating. He was about to offer to rent the property when the owner said he would only pay $5.00 an hour for Clayton to fix it up, and so began Clayton's long sojourn at the former Miwok settlement. He always thought he shared Laird's Landing with the spirits of the Indians who had lived there years before, and that the place was haunted by benevolent ghosts.

One day Clayton's son, Tom, found a large net in the bushes at Laird's Landing. It was a beach seine net. They decided to try it. To their amazement they pulled in hundreds of pounds of perch, a fish too bony to eat. Clayton discovered that Chinese cooks like to use

perch to make fish stock, so he started trucking perch, herring and other varieties of fish to Chinatown. Joe Slatterly, his fishing partner, said they never made a lot of money but those times with Clayton were wonderful. "He was amazing. When he rowed out to the boat, he never looked behind him to see where he was going. It was all instinctive and he was always right. Going fishing with Clayton was very healing. He would talk about how wondrous it was on the bay and he would let go any fish we couldn't use."

Richard and I went down to Laird's Landing at dawn to watch Clayton and Joe fish. They had no luck that day but Richard took some beautifully images of them working together. "I'm the only person who caught anything!" he told them.

Clayton loved taking people on adventures, literally and figuratively. At his last birthday party, he was about to take folks home across the bay in his naval launch when Robin Zank mentioned that although she had lived in Inverness for 15 years she had never actually been on Tomales Bay. "A Tomales Bay Virgin," Clayton said, "We'll have to do something about that." So Robin climbed in the boat with about 20 other people. "The boat was

One end of the net is staked to the shore. Clayton and Joe then row in a semi – circle further along the beach, throwing out the 400 feet of net as they go. White floats hold the net up while the bottom is weighted. When they reach the shore they both pull in the net. The fish try to swim out to sea as the net surrounds them. In the middle of the net is an opening into which the fish swim, believing it to be a hole; but a long bag of mesh streaming behind catches them.

PULLING THE NET

INSPECTING THE CATCH IN THE NET

CLAYTON'S ANCHOR
Laird's Landing

pretty full and when we got to Marshall everybody ducked down so Clayton could see. He had poor eyesight by then, but Clayton was so experienced, docking was no problem. It was dark by the time we got back to Laird's Landing and it was a beautiful ride. I could not have asked for a better introduction to the bay."

Clayton himself had such an open spirit that he attracted people of all descriptions to him. What they had in common, was reverence for the Earth and an irreverence for authority. On occasion Clayton found ways to express this irreverence creatively. A few years ago feral pigs were seen around Point Reyes National Seashore and people became extremely worried. Clayton thought the concern was getting out of hand. He and his friend, Richard Kirschman, did some research and discovered what a wild pig's tracks looked like. Clayton then carved wooden clogs with tracks on the soles. He wore them on the beach, made beautiful tracks for a 3000-pound feral pig, photographed them, and submitted the picture to the Point Reyes Light where it was duly published!

Another day a friend, Mary Moser, paddled in a canoe to visit. By the time she wanted to leave, the wind had

picked up so Clayton decided to rig up a sail for her. He jury rigged a mast in the canoe and attached an improvised sail. "I sailed home, holding the end of the sail and using a paddle as a rudder. It was very efficient and I got back really quickly!"

A raven grew tame at Laird's Landing, and Clayton called him Never More. The raven would sit on Clayton's head and he would talk to him. If Clayton was working on a project and could not pay attention to Never More, the bird would swoop down, take Clayton's hat in his beak and fly off with it.

Eventually Never More found a mate whom he brought back to Laird's Landing for a short visit before taking off forever.

It was Clayton's dream for Laird's Landing to become a place of learning and retreat for artists and environmentalists of all ages. After his death, the Clayton Lewis Institute for Art and Ecology was formed to try and actualize his dream. They were unsuccessful in making Laird's Landing the center Clayton had visualized. However, as a result of their efforts some of the buildings will be saved and stabilized. Clayton, the artist, and his predecessors, the Coast Miwok, will be remembered. Perhaps an artist-in-residence program will be started at Point Reyes National Seashore in recognition of the role artists have played in bringing the beauty of parks to the public. The environmental education program which periodically gives demonstrations on the use of the beach seine continues to this day. To find out more about this program, please write to the Clayton Lewis Institute, P. O. Box 764, Marshall, CA 94940.

CLAYTON IN HIS STUDIO

On the envelope:
Rosie Baldwin   751   Kearney Street
Port Townsend   Wa

USA 20
Solar energy / Knoxville World's Fair

SELF PORTRAIT FOR ROSIE   7/82

*O*ne of a series of paintings on envelopes that Clayton created for his mother who was living in a nursing home in Port Townsend. He was unable to visit her as much as he would have liked so he sent her almost daily letters with illustrated envelopes. He would incorporate the design of the stamp into his picture. They were first exhibited in a gallery in Paris.

OYSTERS

Famed for both their exquisite taste and aphrodisiac qualities, oysters were in such demand in Rome about 100 A.D. that on their journey from the shores of England, elephants were used to transport oysters, packed in ice, across the Alps.

Oysters are still very popular though nowadays their journey to the local restaurants and markets is not too long. West Marin is a major source of the oysters on the half-shell eaten in the bay area. They are farmed in the pristine waters of Tomales Bay and Drakes Estero.

Native to Tomales Bay is the Olympia oyster or ostrea lurida. Popular in the 1800's when the oysters in San Francisco Bay were eaten almost to extinction, the Olympia is now not usually considered commercially viable as it is both small and slow growing. Eastern or pacific oysters were introduced to San Francisco Bay in 1896 by Mr. M. B. Moraghan when he planted an over-supply of oysters he had imported. The oysters grew and multiplied and a new local business was born.

Mr. Moraghan also planted oyster beds in Tomales Bay in 1906 and founded the Tomales Bay Oyster Company. He obtained a permit for harvesting oysters from Tomales Bay in 1909. These oysters became increasingly important as San Francisco grew more populated and its bay became polluted. In 1936 the last commercial oysters were harvested from San Francisco Bay. The Tomales Bay Oyster Company, now owned by Gretchen and Drew Alden and their partners, is still in the business of farming Pacific oysters.

Japanese oysters were introduced to Tomales Bay in 1928. Four years later they were planted in Drakes Estero which proved to be an ideal growing environment.

The water in both Tomales Bay and Drakes Estero is too cold to allow natural spawning of oysters other than those native to the area. Farmers buy seed oysters and grow them using methods which vary depending on the desired end product. If the oyster will be sold shucked, it does not matter if it is grown in a cluster. In this case the oyster larvae are introduced into tanks containing oyster or clam shells and water from the bay. After a week, the new oysters are small black dots attached to a mother shell. These shells are hung on racks in the bay either in mesh bags or strings of 100 shells. Two months later, they are taken from the bay and strung, 14 shells to eight feet of wire, and again hung on the racks in the bay. After 18 to 24 months, they are harvested and sold as shucked bottled oysters or as oysters in the shell. Johnson's Oyster Company have been farming Pacific oysters in this way in Drakes Estero. They lease over 1100 acres from the Department of Fish and Game.

To produce oysters on the half shell, another approach is needed to avoid growing clusters. The farmer buys seed from a hatchery which grinds the oyster shell into 300 micron chips so there is only room for one larvae on each chip. The hatchery grows them for one or two months until the oysters are about 1/4 inch long. Then they are sold to the farmer who places the single seed oysters in fine plastic mesh screen trays, suspended in water. When the oysters reach an inch in size, they are transferred into heavy plastic mesh bags, tied to metal racks that keep the bags floating free in the tidal waters of the bay. Eighteen months later they are harvested. Four other types of oysters are grown in Tomales Bay: kumamoto, euroflat, atlantic or eastern, and olympia. These oysters prefer to grow lying in the mud and mature in three years. Oysters feed on plankton and nutrient and play an important part in keeping Tomales Bay clean.

THE EATING OF OYSTERS

The best introduction to shucking oysters is observing a professional oyster shucker so you can learn their tricks. Failing that, follow our tips. First of all, protect your hands with heavy gloves or a cloth so that you don't cause yourself a mortal injury - the danger is the knife slipping and stabbing you in the hand. Use a good oyster knife, never a kitchen knife. Slip and pry the oyster knife into the beak or deep end of the oyster while holding the shell with the other hand. Cut the muscle which holds the oyster closed by inserting the oyster knife about 2/3 of the way to the other end of the oyster and sliding the blade back and forth until the shell opens. Then cut the oyster free of the shell by cutting the muscle on the other side. Rinse any shell fragments. If you have no luck, putting the oyster in a microwave for a short time will help.

HALF–SHELL OYSTERS WITH TOBIKO AND CREAM

My favorite way to eat oysters is *on the half shell*, flavored with a squirt of lemon and a dash of hot sauce. Served like this, oysters have a purity of taste and fresh texture which I find hard to improve upon.

Breakfast is the time to savor a *Hangtown fry*. It is an omelette filled with sauteed oysters and bacon. Tradition has it that this omelette got its name as the most popular last meal requested by prisoners awaiting hanging. They knew they could gain a few more days by asking for oysters in the Sierra goldfields. Barbequed oysters is another choice. Put oysters on the half shell on a grill and cover them with barbeque sauce and a dab of butter. Alternatively, put the scrubbed but closed oyster on the grill until it is easy to open (with oven mitts) then drop a small dab of butter into the shell, add some sauce. We like them with Everett & Jones sauce from Oakland.

THE FISH DOCK AT CHIMNEY ROCK

The Point Reyes Peninsula is flanked by a highly productive area of the ocean. Upwelling of nutriments and the Cordell Bank provide a perfect habitat for many fish species. Fishing fleets are based in Bodega Bay while there are moorings and a fish dock near Chimney Rock.

Chef Margaret Grade of Manka's assembled this platter of local fish and seafood. Featured are salmon roe, clams, mussels, trout and Dungeness crab.

FARMING ON THE MARIN COAST

COWS, CLIFFS AND DRAKES BAY FROM GEORGE NUNES' FARM

SPALETTA DAIRY AND POINT REYES

THE IMPORTANCE OF FARMS

West Marin is famous for the idyllic beauty of its rolling hills and long panoramic landscapes, occasionally dotted with farm buildings.

The land with its rich pasture is ideal for dairy farming unlike the area further south which is covered with chaparral while the north is forested.

Outside West Marin's small towns and villages, urban life does not spread along the highway gradually petering out to a country scene. This is not a happy accident rather the result of hard work by hundreds of environmentalists who battled developers and legislators tooth and nail.

In 1962 President John F. Kennedy authorized the establishment of Point Reyes National Seashore, 53,000 acres along the Pacific coast. This land included thousands of acres of farmland. It was however crucial to West Marin farming that the farms within the park continue to operate because dairy farms require a certain minimum number of active farms in an area to remain economically viable. If the number of dairy farms drops below that minimum it is no longer profitable to collect milk and service the farms. As a result the farms within the park were sold to the government and then leased back to their previous owners.

A movement was started to further protect the Marin farmland by restricting its development. The first step, in 1972, was the introduction of a new zoning ordinance, A-60, which said that agricultural land could not be divided into parcels smaller than sixty acres and only one residence could be built on each parcel.

It was a great start to protect open space in Marin but there was still the possibility of farmers selling their land for "ranchettes". These do not live comfortably next to real farms which create dust, smells and flies, not acceptable daily problems for a gentleman farmer. They also tend to raise the price of land beyond the reach of farmers. This would lead to the gradual break down of the agricultural community.

There had to be a permanent solution. There were too many farms for the local government to buy in Marin county. Besides many farmers did not like the idea of giving up owner-

The cows love it here. They love eating the grass and being milked when they are full of milk.
– R.B.

COWS AT GEORGE NUNES' FARM
Near Chimney Rock

FOAL AT STEWART RANCH
Highway One

SQUARE COW BUTTS

ship of their land.

A local rancher, Ellen Straus, and Phyllis Faber, a biologist, proposed creating an agricultural land trust which would buy up the development rights of farms. The farmer would receive cash to invest in their farm, buy more land, take care of estate taxes or pay out siblings for their share in the farm. The land would be safe from developers even if it were sold in the future. In 1980 the Marin Agricultural Land Trust was formed. It is an alliance of ranchers, political leaders and environmentalists. They have to date acquired the agricultural conservation easements on 39 Marin farms and ranches totalling over 26,000 acres. These easements protect over 20% of all privately owned agricultural land in the county!

The ranches within the Point Reyes National Seashore have both individual names and historical names that are designated by a letter of the alphabet. This system was devised during the partnership of Charles Howard and James and Oscar Shafter in 1869 as a way to keep track of their numerous holdings.

Marin produces 25% of the milk for the bay area. Its pastures are considered among the most productive in the U.S., three times more productive than the California average. It takes 6 acres of land on the West Marin coast to support a cow and her calf. In the Central Valley, it may take as much as 20 acres of range.

HORSES GRAZING WITH INVERNESS RIDGE BEYOND

RAINBOW OVER MENDOSA FARM
Point Reyes National Seashore

COW FACE

BARN ALONG HIGHWAY ONE

This structure was recently demolished.

KEHOE RANCH
Pierce Point Road

FARMHOUSE NEAR MARIN/SONOMA BORDER
This structure was recently renovated.

FARM ARCHITECTURE

Farmers know the land and weather patterns and use this knowledge when deciding the location and design of farm buildings. This feeling for the landscape informs the barn design process; the farmer wants practicality and efficiency as well. Functional designs are often the most evolved and their simple shapes and weathered exteriors that blend with the land, really add to the beauty of West Marin while providing a visual link to the early history of the area. Axel Nelson, a local contractor, who restored a barn in Bolinas, thought that crews of carpenters went farm–to–farm building barns. Pierce Point Ranch in the park has been restored and is such a classic example of barn design and construction which many have copied.

West Marin is a harsh environment for buildings. Most of the structures built during the settlement era have disappeared without a trace, except in vintage photographs. Some burned, water and salty air rotted many, others were torn down.

We love farm architecture and have designed our house to echo that style. Over time it will look like an old barn and fit into the landscape.

BARN IN THE MIST

SIDING & WINDOW
Hicks Valley

FARMHOUSE, "A" RANCH

ROCK WALL & GATE
Mendosa Ranch

BARN AT GOSPEL FLATS
Bolinas
Recently restored

IMMIGRATION TO WEST MARIN

Intertwined with the history of the farms in West Marin are the lives of immigrants, many from Switzerland and Mexico. The Swiss started arriving in California in the 1850's. Originally attracted by the gold fever engulfing the area, they soon moved back to their roots of farming, and more particularly, dairy farming. With its natural rich pasture land, West Marin was ideal. Today thirty percent of the ranch land in Marin is owned by descendants of these immigrants.

In 1964 Carmelo Hermosillo, a field worker from Jalostotitlan, a town in central Mexico, landed a job on a dairy ranch near the Sonoma/Marin border. Unlike most farm jobs, it was not seasonal. Hermosillo wrote to his family telling of the availability of permanent jobs in the area. As a result a steady stream of people from "Jalos" as it is affectionately called, started making their way to West Marin.

As the years went by and the men were joined by their families, the Mexican immigrants have had a profound affect on West Marin. Many children who live in this area are bilingual. Farm workers are branching out and starting their own businesses. Fiestas are held in which all sectors of the community participate.

Traditionally in Mexico, when a girl turns fifteen she has a formal coming-out ceremony, called a quinceañera. It is a combination of a service during which the girl is accepted into the church as an adult, and a celebration similar to a debutante's ball. Richard (as the photographer) and I were invited to the quinceañera of Yesenia Padilla. We had no idea it would be such an elaborate occasion. The ceremony began in the Sacred Heart Church in Olema. The church was filled. Not only was fifteen year old Yesenia celebrating her quinceañera, but her parents, Gloria and Carmelo Padilla, were reconfirming their marriage vows. The service was accompanied by a mariachi band. Yesenia had 50 attendants of all ages. The girls wore emerald green or dark pink satin while their partners wore tuxedos with matching bow ties and cummerbunds.

Afterwards we all went to the home of Gloria and her family at "A" ranch where Carmelo is the ranch foreman. Tables had been laid out in the farmyard and 250 people sat down for a wonderful meal accompanied by music from the mariachi band. Next came traditional Mexican dancing. The celebration continued with a barn dance in a real barn with a rock and roll band. Finally the eight tiered cake was cut. It was a truly memorable event.

YESENIA PADILLA AND HUMBERTO "BETO" RICO

Latinos often work jobs that many would not take, because of the physical labor, low pay and inherently dangerous farm machinery they operate. Their lack of native English, plus hostility from bigots, sometimes limits their opportunities. However, hard work, intelligence and strong family support are constantly improving the prospects of Latinos. Make no mistake, when you sit down to eat, whether at home or in a restaurant, many of the hands which grew and prepared your food were Latino. Please support and honor their strenuous efforts to succeed. Everybody benefits from mutual respect and understanding.

The Straus Family Creamery is a pioneer dairy farm and creamery. Bill Straus began farming in 1941 with 23 cows named after his friends and relatives. As the years continued, the farm grew. Along the way a strong commitment to environmental sustainability guided decisions made on the farm. Bill's wife, Ellen, was one of the architects of the Marin Agricultural Land Trust, (MALT) which buys the development rights of farms. In 1994 the farm, led by Albert, Bill's oldest son, became the first certified organic dairy west of the Mississippi. It took three years for the land on their 660 acre farm to be certified. After obtaining this designation, their herd of cattle had to be fed organic grain for a year before their milk could be sold as organic. They keep the herd small to maintain the health of both the cows and the land. Straus milk is sold in glass bottles which are reused by the creamery an average of 8 times. The milk is not homogenized so the cream floats naturally to the top. Shake the milk before pouring or follow our routine of skimming off the cream for our coffee in the morning. Their milk is pasteurized to kill harmful bacteria. They use no sprays, pesticides or chemical fertilizers and their cows are never treated with hormones or genetic growth factors to increase milk production. The Straus Family Creamery sells milk, yogurt, butter and cheese throughout California.

Over twenty years ago Warren Weber bought 100 acres of land just outside Bolinas. He turned it into an organic farm, Star Route Farms. He grows organic greens and vegetables next to a public school. Organic farms can be safely located next to towns. Other organic farms have sprung up, like Peter Martinelli's Paradise Valley Ranch

which his family have owned for 65 years. Peter has 18 acres under cultivation and produces a wide variety of organically grown vegetables, fruit and flowers which he markets under the Fresh Run Farm name. "When I need help, I try and find aspiring career farmers who want to learn and deal with all the problems, stresses and satisfaction of organic farming" said Peter.

Tomales Bay Foods, run by food mavens Sue Conley and Peggy Smith, is in a renovated barn in Point Reyes Station. Sue formerly managed the renowned Bette's Diner in Berkeley while Peggy was a head chef at Chez Panisse! Part of the operation is the Cowgirl Creamery which makes various organic cheeses, creme fraiche, quark and ice cream. Tomales Bay Foods celebrates the extraordinary quality of foods grown in West Marin. Many speciality organic producers market their products through the store which sells both fresh produce and perfectly cooked and seasoned food using local ingredients. It's a win-win situation. The farmer has a market and the store provides food creations based on the freshest and healthiest ingredients.

It's a strangely moving experience to taste local food. When you love the food you're getting from farms and sea, you want to help protect the bio-systems from pollution or development. Richard swears that he can taste the same flavor in a Tomales Bay oyster that he tastes when swimming in Tomales Bay. In many parts of the country, people have lost this farm to table connection. Co-existence with farms is essential for quality of life.

PARADISE VALLEY RANCH
Bolinas

Dairy products of West Marin include
eggs, cheese, butter and milk.

ARRANGEMENT BY MARGARET GRADE
MANKA'S INVERNESS LODGE

Morel and porcini mushrooms, carrots,
basil, blackberries, artichokes, and kale

ARRANGEMENT BY MARGARET GRADE
MANKA'S INVERNESS LODGE

RANCH REFLECTED IN NICASIO RESERVOIR

During the summer a Farmers' Market is held every Saturday morning outside Toby's Feed Barn in Point Reyes.

A new product being grown in the county is olives. The McEvoy Ranch on the Point Reyes/Petaluma Road has planted over 10,000 olive trees, consisting of six varieties native to Tuscany. In 1995 they harvested their first organic olives and made olive oil using traditional methods.

OLIVE GROVES

Manka's Restaurant in Inverness nurtures its guests in a turn-of-the-century hunting lodge where local food and wild game are on the menu. Margaret Grade, the chef and owner, creates an atmosphere of the arts and crafts era. She and her staff amaze their guests with gourmet meals that are made from over 70% local ingredients. Manka's ambiance is transforming because of the depth and breath of the virtual stage the restaurant has become. Its immersive experience of culture, wine, and exquisite food is a journey into Margaret Grades' utopian dream world. Floral excess abounds. Friends of ours, Robin Zank and Matthew Prebluda, of the Knave of Hearts Bakery, made the bread for Manka's. They told Margaret they would be bringing Matthew's father, Irving, for dinner. When they arrived, the top of the menu read, in Manka's own typeface: "For our VIP guests, Matt, the missus and his father". They had their own waiter and were placed next to Robert Redford. Seeing all the attention our friends were getting, Mr. Redford asked his waiter who the big shots were! Another evening we brought in a huge wild mushroom we had found on our land. Margaret identified it, pronounced it one of the finest for flavor, then cooked it in a cream sauce. Fabulous!

We can't list everyone who deserves credit for locally grown food or thank all our talented chefs, but all are deserving of praise. May their numbers multiply!

NICASIO FARM

BARNWOOD RETURNING TO SOIL

OCEAN LIGHT FROM MOUNT TAMALPAIS

Overlooking San Francisco Bay and Marin County, Mount Tamalpais was thought by the Miwok Indians to be the home of their god, Coyote. They considered it a place of reverence.

The first recorded ascent of Mount Tamalpais was made in the 1830's by a trader, Jacob Leese. He wanted to establish an initial survey point on its peak but his Indian assistants refused to accompany him. They thought nobody would survive a visit to the sacred summit. When Leese returned unscathed, Chief Marin, after whom the county is named, climbed to the top and enhanced his reputation among his people as the bravest man in the world.

STINSON BEACH AND BOLINAS, SUNSET

According to linguists, the name, Tamalpais, is a combination of the Miwok words "tamal", meaning coast or west and "pais", meaning hill. It is also sometimes known as the "sleeping princess."

It is not a huge mountain, 2,604 feet to the peak, but Mount Tamalpais rises directly from the beach in the west and the San Francisco Bay in the east. In 1896 a railway track was built from Mill Valley to the summit. During its first year of operation the Mount Tamalpais Scenic Railroad carried 23,000 passengers up its 8 mile track. At the end of the track was a luxury hotel. When the railway was extended to include Muir Woods, the downward trip was made into a gravity ride; no engine was needed but lots of braking force was applied. It was reputedly an exciting ride, not as fast as a roller coaster, but still quite a thrill. The motor car proved too fierce a competitor for the train and in 1930, the railroad was closed while the hotel was demolished in the 1950s. The track is now a hiking trail.

Most of the trees on Mount Tamalpais were logged between 1840 and 1870. Fortunately one stand of redwoods in Sequoia Canyon was fairly inaccessible and was left untouched. In 1905 the canyon was for sale and it seemed inevitable it, too, would be logged. William Kent, a conservationist and land developer who owned much of the area, wanted the Mount Tamalpais Park Association to buy the canyon. They could not raise the money so he bought it himself. He deeded it to the United States government but it was still not out of danger. Two years later a local water company wanted the canyon floor condemned for a reservoir. Kent appealed to the President of the United States, Theodore Roosevelt sending him photographs of the redwoods to make

OAK BRANCH, MARIN HEADLANDS & SAN FRANCISCO
From Dad O'Rourke Bench, Mt Tamalpais

SAN FRANCISCO PANORAMA FROM MOUNT TAMALPAIS

LACY WATERFALL, FALL COLORS
Cascade Creek

his case. Roosevelt declared Sequoia Canyon a National Monument and named it Muir Woods.

Mount Tamalpais was originally inhabited by mountain lion, bobcats, black and grizzly bear, coyote, elk and deer. The last recorded bear was caught in a trap in Muir Woods in 1880. Mountain lion are still very occasionally sighted on the mountain. Hunting was a popular pastime until Mount Tamalpais was declared a game reserve in 1917. This did not affect the large watersheds of the Big and Little Carson Creeks where hunting continued until 1971 when the Marin Municipal Water District cancelled the lease of the Redwood Gun Club.

The Marin Municipal Water District, established in 1912, bought up the drainage of Lagunitas Creek east and north of Tamalpais. Kent gave additional land at Muir Woods, a right–of–way easement for the Panoramic Highway and 200 acres at Steep Ravine. In 1930, with land bought by the Mount Tamalpais Park Association and the state, Mount Tamalpais became a State Park, the first state park in California. Over the years its boundaries have been extended until, in 1973, the National Park Service bought more land to bring the park to its present size of 6,301 acres.

MATT ECSTATIC ON MOUNT TAMALPAIS
Dad O'Rourke Bench

Thousands of hikers enjoy over 200 miles of trails on Mount Tamalpais, which wind through redwoods, chaparral and grasslands. Some years its slopes are covered with masses of lupine and California poppies. Over 700 varieties of plants have been counted. The circular path near the summit has panoramic views which extend from San Francisco and the Bay Area to the Pacific Ocean and Napa County.

It is possible for the entire bay area to be cloaked in thick fog when high on Mount Tamalpais are blue skies and sunshine. One is floating over a layer of clouds feeling sorry for the shivering millions below.

CASCADE CREEK

*Mount Tamalpais has a lush, green environment of streams in
tree–shaded canyons through which brooks run. By Cascade
Creek is a trail from Rock Meadows down to Alpine Lake. It
is particularly beautiful in the fall and spring.*

Many of the trails, bridges and present day picnic sites on Mount Tamalpais were constructed or significantly improved by the Civilian Conservation Corps started in 1933 to provide jobs during the depression. The CCC was also primarily responsible for building the Mountain Theatre. Five thousand boulders weighing from 600 to 4000 pounds were brought in and buried in rows so that only a small portion of their bulk showed. A massive rock wall with interlocking boulders made a level stage. Chinkapin and natural vegetation was planted to serve as entrances and to screen behind stage activities. The amphitheater seats 4,000 and hosts 6 performances every year.

Mount Tamalpais is the shining summit of the bay area and west Marin.

MOUNT SAINT HELENA FROM MOUNT TAMALPAIS

CLASSIC HIKES OF WEST MARIN

HIKING TO COAST CAMP ON THE BLUFFS ABOVE LIMANTOUR BEACH

VIEW SOUTH FROM MILLER POINT
Also known as Arch Rock, Point Reyes National Seashore.

BEAR VALLEY TO MILLER POINT (ARCH ROCK)

Layers of green surround the hiker on the Bear Valley Trail which winds its way through a forest, past a meadow, and ends at Arch Rock on the Pacific Ocean. Overhanging branches from bay trees form giant arches over the path edged with sword ferns, forget-me-nots, sorrel and richly diverse vegetation. Bear Valley Creek runs alongside the path until it reaches Divide Meadow.

BEAR VALLEY CREEK

Formerly the site of a hunting lodge, Divide Meadow is now a favorite grazing spot for deer. Bear Valley was named for the large number of grizzly bears that roamed in the area before they were hunted to extinction early in the twentieth century.

After Divide Meadow, Coast Creek flows along the trail. Small streams running down the canyon join the creek. At the ocean, particularly in the spring, it is fast flowing and a challenge to cross. Alders line the banks of the creek forming a canopy under which the water travels. Ferns grow mysteriously out of the branches of the moss covered bay trees. Douglas iris, bleeding hearts and buttercups provide splashes of contrasting color in the palette of varying shades of green.

Four miles down the trail is the ocean and Arch Rock, a promontory which juts out to sea, giving a panoramic view of the coast. North is Chimney Rock, Drakes Beach, Limantour Beach and Sculptured Beach. To the south, Alamere Falls and Double Point can be seen on a clear day. Below, waves crash against the rocks while pelican and cormorant perch on salty sea stacks. Seals and very occasionally, whales can sometimes be observed cavorting in the swell.

There is a path down the side of Coast Creek. It is a tricky path past patches of poison oak and, at the bottom, one must hop rocks to reach the other side. There you see the stream going through the rock. *Only* during a low tide can you follow Coast Creek through the arch and access a beach. It is also possible to reach the small beach south of Arch Rock. The combination of high tide and a Pacific storm brings spectacular waves crashing through the arch.

COAST CREEK THROUGH THE ARCH
Miller Point

FLOWERS, CLIFFS AND FOG
Chimney Rock Trail

AERIAL VIEW OF CHIMNEY ROCK

CHIMNEY ROCK

Unbelievable wildflowers, dramatic landscapes, elephant seals (at a distance), a historical lifesaving station, an active commercial fishing dock and a possible haunt of romantic poets, this trail is one of the finest short hikes in the United States. It is also home to the rare Mission Bell flower near the end of Chimney Rock.

To reach the trail head, take the road towards the Point Reyes Lighthouse then take the left fork to Chimney Rock. The path follows the ridge and goes to the aptly named rock formation at the southern tip of the Point Reyes headlands. After 1/2 mile atop a hill, a side trail branches off to the right and leads to a spectacular view of the cliffs and Pacific Ocean. On the isolated cliffs between Chimney Rock and the lighthouse many seals, sea lions and elephant seals lie 'hauled out' on the beach. The sandy shore offers a place to rest, provides a respite from the sharks, and allows the pinnipeds to warm themselves, mate and raise pups in season. The park service has closed the area to let these wild sea creatures live undisturbed. A good general rule of thumb for photographers and observers is to not change the behavior of the subject. If the animal becomes frightened and moves away, one has come too close.

Back on the trail, the hike is rich in wildflowers during spring. In winter the overlooks offer prime whale watching, particularly February through March when the grey whale mothers and their calves travel close to the shore as they return from Baja, Mexico on their way back to Alaska.

Since Point Reyes has a reputation for being the foggiest and windiest place on the Pacific coast, we suggest bringing warm clothes and wind proof jackets. There is some poison oak but not much. The total hike to Chimney Rock and back is less than two miles with relatively minor changes in elevation. We would rate this hike as moderately easy while the views gained are second to none.

CHIMNEY ROCK FROM END OF TRAIL

SAM GOLDBERG IN AN ANGELIC STATE

ALAMERE FALLS
Palomarin Trail

ALAMERE FALLS FROM PALOMARIN

Alamere Falls is a spectacular waterfall which flows into the Pacific Ocean after the winter rains. The 11 mile round trip hike to the falls starts at the Palomarin Trailhead, near Bolinas, and follows the coast trail past two beautiful lakes, Bass and Pelican.

There are great views of the ocean and lush canyons to traverse. The elevation gain and loss is moderate but it's a relatively long day hike so one needs to get an early start. Bring warm clothes for possible fog and a flashlight in case of a late return journey. The area is covered with poison oak and long pants might come in handy.

There are two ways to get to the beach by the waterfall. The most direct is a path just south of the falls. It involves a bit of a scramble down a rocky slope. One member on our hike had a fear of heights so we took the alternative route, hiking well north of the falls, near Wildcat Camp, reaching the falls via the shore.

There is something primal about seeing water return in such a dramatic manner to the sea. It combines two favorite forms of nature: waterfalls and ocean surf. Camping at Wildcat on a fog free full moon night in the spring and visiting the falls at night would be a memorable experience.

Another way to reach Alamere Falls is from the Five Brooks trailhead. This involves climbing over Firtop, 1300 feet high, a round trip means a 2600 feet elevation gain. Bikes are allowed on this route to nearby Wildcat Beach, but it's a hard trip back. Richard likes to say the bike ride there was "a once in a lifetime experience" because it was so hard to go back he isn't likely to repeat it.

POISON OAK

AERIAL VIEW OF BASS AND CRYSTAL LAKES
Palomarin trail

HIKING TIPS

☞ Bring warm windproof clothing during any season as unexpected fog and wind can cause hypothermia. Goretex and fleece are ideal.

☞ Carry a flashlight, matches, water and a tide guide. Many hikers are trapped between surf and cliffs as the tide rises.

☞ Never turn your back on the ocean. People have been swept out to sea by sneaker waves.

☞ Learn to identify poison oak and stinging nettles.

☞ Tell friends and/or family members or the National Park Service rangers your route if your plans are potentially hazardous.

☞ Remember, enjoyment is the keynote; let the slower members of your group set the pace.

TOMALES POINT TRAIL

AERIAL VIEW OF TOMALES POINT
K. P. Goodwin

Of all the hikes in West Marin, a walker on the trail to Tomales Point is most likely to be rewarded with the sight of wildlife. This area of the park is home to six herds of tule elk. On a recent trip to the point, I saw three herds of tule elk, an ermine, a bobtail rabbit, a vole, two deer, vultures, pelicans, cormorants, seagulls, sea lion, and a great egret. It's about 11 miles to the point round trip.

The trail begins at the restored buildings of the Pierce Point Ranch, one of the original dairy farms in the area. An interest in farm architecture could make this a destination in itself. The trail goes up and down grass covered hills until Tomales Point is reached. Here the land seems to slide into the ocean at the confluence of Tomales Bay and the Pacific. On the ocean side are deeply eroded canyons with layers of different colored sand reminiscent of Death Valley. Towards Tomales Bay you will see Hog Island and idyllic beaches. Across the bay is Tom's Point where oysters, clams and abalone are farmed. South is McClure's Rock, the Great Beach, and finally the Point Reyes Headlands.

The path is lined with wild radish, yellow, white, and pale lilac. Yellow lupine cover the ridge top, interspersed with hemlock, mustard, California poppies, cockle burrs and wild yarrow.

The view from Tomales Point is spectacular with pelicans whizzing by crashing waves, barking sea lions, mingling currents, tidal rips and sneaker waves. Beyond the maelstrom is Dillon Beach, sand dunes, Bodega Head, the Sonoma Coast, and on a clear day, Mount St. Helena.

Near the end of the trail a buoy sounds like the peal of a church bell. It guides sailors at the mouth of Tomales Bay which is notorious for sneaker waves and shoals. At the point, a worn rope marks a steep and dangerous rappel down to the beach. Divers sometimes search for abalone near the entrance to the Bay; a risky venture, as it is the breeding ground for great white sharks and divers have been attacked. So, don't get eaten or fall off a cliff holding what is left of the rope, just enjoy the view and return safely.

PIERCE POINT FARMHOUSE
Tomales Point Trail

ELK AND SPARKLING SEA
Tomales Point Trail

SCENES OF WONDER & CURIOSITY IN WEST MARIN

OSPREYS NESTING ON POWER POLE
Tomales Bay & Highway One

These birds and their nest were moved by biologists and PG&E crews to a new pole in an elaborate procedure which involved transporting the nest with a crane and temporarily substituting eggs in the nest to protect the real eggs from breakage. However the birds moved on.

SCENES OF WONDER AND CURIOSITY

Perhaps there are other areas in America where the locals celebrate the Harvest moon en masse but in my travels I have never seen such celebrations advertised in the local newspaper. This is how I learned of the picnic on top of Mount Vision to watch the rise of the Harvest Moon over Elephant Mountain (also known as Black Mountain depending on whom you talk to).

About 100 people showed up on a warm late summer evening carrying picnic baskets and rugs. It was difficult to know where to look. The view east was compelling as one did not want to miss the

PIPER ON THE RIDGE
Mount Vision looking west

moment the yellow moon peeked over the striking silhouette of Elephant Mountain. On the other hand, the sun was setting below waves of fog over the Pacific Ocean. The crest of the fog picked up glorious shades of orange and red making an exquisite blanket. In the midst of the spectacular beauty the bagpiper, Dan McNear, started blowing and the haunting sounds of Scottish pipes filled the air of Inverness, California.

Afterwards I headed home, taking the Inverness Ridge trail. Aided by the full moon, I used my flashlight only when walking through the shade of the Bishop Pine forest. The occasional hooting of an owl and the chirp of a bird I awoke, kept me company.

INVERNESS is sometimes considered a somewhat staid place which leaves wild happenings to Bolinas but for many years on the Fourth of July, Inverness let loose. Townsfolk would pack up picnic baskets, wood for camp-fires, plenty of fireworks and head for Drakes Beach. The first time I witnessed the celebration I was astounded.

People were hauling huge logs on to the beach for their bonfires and carrying giant coolers filled with gourmet food and drinks. This was beach partying on a level I had never before encountered. Park Rangers walked down the beach at 6 pm, telling everyone that fireworks and drinking were not allowed on park property. Their audience nodded solemnly.

As dusk approached, the volley ball nets were put away and the camp fires started in earnest. There must have been at least 25 fires extending up and down the beach. People would wander from one fire to the next to join friends for a chat and refreshments. A sailboat even arrived and anchored offshore. They had sailed from Sausalito. The crew jumped into a dinghy and joined the party.

Now it was dark and the fireworks began. Rockets with multiple explosions, Catherine wheels, hundreds of sparklers and then in the midst of all this a lone bagpiper started playing his pipes on the cliffs above the beach. It was like a scene from an ancient battlefield - the bagpipes, the fires, the smell of gunpowder, the shouting and laugh-ter of people running around lit by the flames of the fires.

Unfortunately the word got out that Drakes Beach was the place to go for July 4th and rowdy crowds started show-ing up from all over. The Park Service could no longer turn a blind eye to the Inverness town party. Now, for good rea-son, Drakes Beach is closed at eight pm the night of July 4th. Local stalwarts still celebrate Independence Day but they keep their whereabouts close to the chest.

★ ✪ ★ ✪ ★ ✪ ★

THE TOMALES BAY SWIM

Once a year hardy residents of West Marin take to the water at Shell Beach for a swim across Tomales Bay *and back*. Richard and I did it for the first time in 1996. I wore a wet suit cap (in addition to my swimsuit) for warmth. Lacking a little confidence in our ability to stay the course I asked a canoeist accompanying the swimmers to keep an eye on us. She did her job faithfully even though we were the last out of the water. The conditions were ideal, sunny weather, the bay like a lake and the tide only coming in strongly the last quarter mile of the return journey. With the boaters keeping watch over us, we could relax and enjoy the swim. We encountered hundreds of jellyfish but of the benevolent persuasion so after a while it actually became an interesting sensual experience to swim through the rubber like creatures. At the end of the swim, a wonderful pancake breakfast with fresh fruit and coffee awaited us on the beach.

1998 was the twenty fifth anniversary of the swim. Due to safety problems like having enough boats to help swimmers, strong currents which put swimmers off course and oblivious speedboats, organizers of this event ask that it remain for locals only as too many swimmers would overwhelm the support system. You can try swimming across Tomales Bay another time with the aid of responsible boaters and pancake chefs!

THE PLUNGE – START OF THE SWIM
Tomales Bay
Photograph by Jan Watson

TWENTY FIFTH ANNIVERSARY CARD
Design and 5 color letterpress printing by
M. Kate St.Clair, Zanni Press, Point Reyes Station

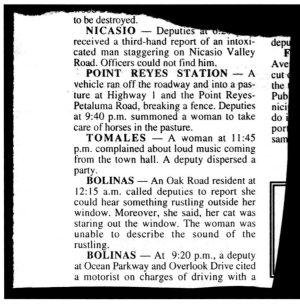

to be destroyed.
NICASIO — Deputies at 6:2... received a third-hand report of an intoxicated man staggering on Nicasio Valley Road. Officers could not find him.
POINT REYES STATION — A vehicle ran off the roadway and into a pasture at Highway 1 and the Point Reyes-Petaluma Road, breaking a fence. Deputies at 9:40 p.m. summoned a woman to take care of horses in the pasture.
TOMALES — A woman at 11:45 p.m. complained about loud music coming from the town hall. A deputy dispersed a party.
BOLINAS — An Oak Road resident at 12:15 a.m. called deputies to report she could hear something rustling outside her window. Moreover, she said, her cat was staring out the window. The woman was unable to describe the sound of the rustling.
BOLINAS — At 9:20 p.m., a deputy at Ocean Parkway and Overlook Drive cited a motorist on charges of driving with a

SHERIFF'S CALLS
Point Reyes Light

This is a sample of the Sheriff's Calls, a weekly feature in the Point Reyes Light. These cryptic entries are often poignant windows into the ups and downs of rural residents. Crime in West Marin is sparse but things happen. We've noticed that alcohol is regularly involved in domestic violence, driving accidents and store break-ins.

The Point Reyes Light, under the direction of veteran newsman and publisher, Dave Mitchell, has accomplished something that many major newspapers long for; a Pulitzer prize, newspapers' highest honor, awarded for the story of Synanon's descent from rehabilitation center to dangerous cult. Synanon members even placed a rattlesnake in a mailbox in a murder attempt!

The Light is the indispensable source for news of West Marin, artist events, columns and letters to the editor, as well as information on housing leads and other classified advertising by locals. Our area is full of brilliant individualists, many retired, who don't hold back on their opinions and emotions. Writing a letter to the editor of the Light is like merging into the fast lane on the freeway.

DAVE MITCHELL

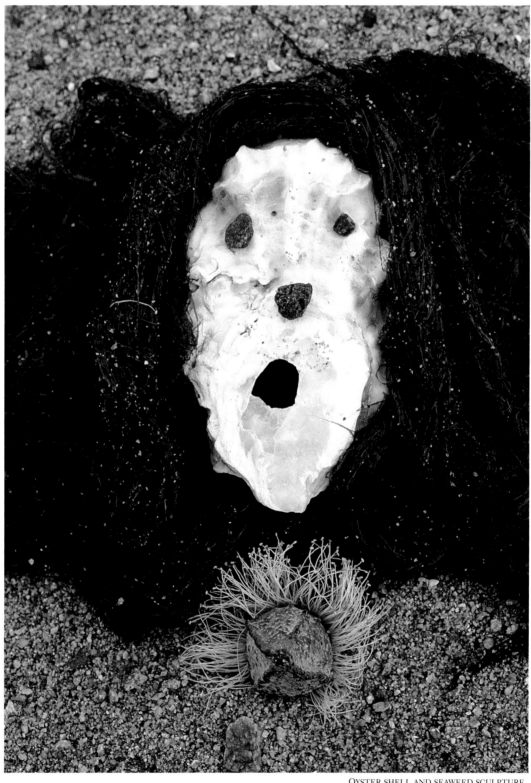

OYSTER SHELL AND SEAWEED SCULPTURE
Teachers Beach, Inverness

Children have the most *wonder and curiosity*. We thank the unknown artist who created this oyster shell face found in the sand.

ENVIRONMENTAL GROUPS OF WEST MARIN

SPIDER WEB WITH MORNING DEW
Inverness Ridge

PLEASE CONTACT THESE environmental groups to protect the wild nature of our national parks, the ocean, and to
preserve ranch land. Hikes, classes, and lectures will increase
your understanding of coastal Marin. You can donate needed
funds and/or volunteer to suit your interests.

AUDUBON CANYON RANCH

The sound of hungry Great Egret chicks fills the canyon. Emerging from the woods, I see an overlook and below, nests atop redwood trees. An adult Great Egret flies overhead. Immediately a crescendo of squawking begins. A couple of chicks start pecking at each other, determined to be first in line when mama or papa delivers the food by regurgitation. When the chicks are newborn, the adult drops the food into the nest but after a couple of weeks, the nestlings figure out the source of their sustenance and as soon as their bills are large enough, at the age of two weeks, they grasp the parent's bill in their own and have a straight transfusion!

number of herons is not diminishing. DDT is on the wane so maybe other places are becoming more hospitable. We are getting Snowy Egrets now. In 1990, a Golden Eagle frightened some herons away and they nested across the lagoon behind Smiley's Bar in Bolinas."

Raccoons raided egret nests in 1975 and heron nests in 1983. They ate all the eggs and young on both occasions which also led to a drop in bird population. The birds started nesting closer together. Staff and volunteers at ACR put metal collars around all the nesting trees and potential nesting trees to prevent raccoons from climbing into the nests again. The raccoons have not returned so far.

ROOKERY AT AUDUBON CANYON RANCH

Audubon Canyon Ranch was founded in 1962 when this major west coast nesting colony for Great Blue Herons, Snowy Egrets and Great Egrets, on the shores of Bolinas Lagoon, was threatened with development. It is a private nonprofit group which owns over 1000 acres adjoining the lagoon, 380 acres of shoreline on Tomales Bay and over 400 acres at the Bouverie Preserve in Sonoma. ACR protects the properties as sanctuaries for native plants and animals. It educates the public and supports research to enhance the preservation and management of the sanctuaries.

The number of breeding pairs of birds at ACR varies from year to year. The Great Blue Herons have gone from a high of 62 pairs in 1968 to the present level of 7 pairs. The resident biologist at ACR, Mr. Ray Peterson said that he was not really concerned at the drop. "When you look at the country as a whole, the

The ACR Preserve on the Bolinas Lagoon is open to the public on weekends and holidays from mid March to mid July. Those interested can visit at other times by appointment. There is a small salaried staff and a large force of volunteers who are either docents or ranch guides. The docents work with school children during the week while the ranch guides educate the public at the weekends. The program is so popular that turnover is low and trainings are not held every year. The ranch guide training takes six weeks while the docent training is spread over 22 weeks. Both groups commit to working at the ranch for a certain amount of time for two years. The ranch is funded almost entirely by public donation. For further information, please call 415 868-9244. Their address is 4900 Highway One, Stinson Beach, CA 94970.

ENVIRONMENTAL ACTION COMMITTEE

The most politically active local environmental group, the Environmental Action Committee of West Marin(EAC), has led legal battles against development of Tomales Bay, the expansion of the West Marin landfill and Santa Rosa's proposed reservoir for treated sewage on the West Marin-Sonoma County lines.

The EAC helped fight successfully all the way to the Supreme Court a developer's challenge to the "A-60" zoning of agricultural land which prohibits the subdivision of agricultural land to less than 60 acres and allows only a single residence to be built on the land.

Founded in 1971, the EAC grew out of a grass roots effort of a few local people concerned that the Tomales Bay wetlands would be turned into a huge housing development. The fight was successful and the small group went on to become a organization supported by 800 members. Former EAC director John Grissim, explained its role.

"West Marin is unincorporated so we have no city council, no real source of government, except our single supervisor's voice, in city hall in San Rafael.We act as a representative of the public trust in issues involving planning, land use, development and conservation of resources. We monitor the planning notices, scrutinize every deal, every development that is coming down the line; we study master plans, and we often appear in front of various boards and agencies that make the decisions. Then we fight the good fight to make sure the zoning laws designed to protect the West Marin green belt are followed. Essentially we always have a good fight on our hands."

A new battle is brewing against the private use of

SEA PALM DETAIL
Great Beach after storm

personal watercraft, like jet skis, in the Gulf of the Farallones National Marine Sanctuary, an area which includes Tomales Bay. "The EAC has petitioned the Department of Commerce to ban them," Grissim said. "We don't know how successful we will be going up against a big industry but we have a good chance."

He added that the reason the EAC had been so successful was because they were not implacably anti-development "We believe we can make partnerships and find a middle ground of all the voices which involves the environmental and the agricultural communities and the developers. Clearly the development pressure on West Marin continues to mount as property values soar. There is so much money available. People are willing to buy 1,000 acres in order to build their trophy home. We feel we will be constantly challenged to defend A-60 zoning from the regularly tried ways found to work around it."

The EAC is active in other arenas. After the 1995 Mount Vision fire, they obtained a grant to create a team of foresters and consultants who published a report on environmental restoration and fire safety procedures. It is considered a national model for fire restoration. They have also produced an half hour video program in Spanish on environmentally conscious living in every day life for California's Latino community. In the summer of 1997 they co-sponsored West Marin's first roadside litter clean up day.

To join or volunteer for the EAC, please call 415 663-9312 or write to the EAC, Box 609, Point Reyes Station, CA 94956.

POINT REYES BIRD OBSERVATORY

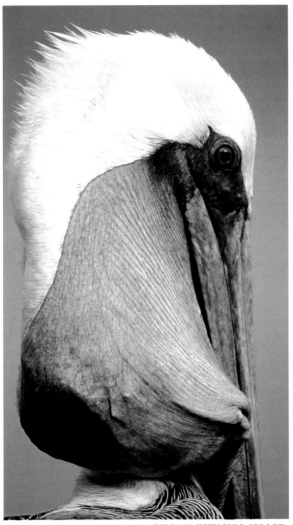

PELICAN WITH FULL GULLET

Key to the protection of bird life in West Marin is the Point Reyes Bird Observatory (PRBO) founded in 1965 as a non-profit membership organization dedicated to pursuing ecological research, interpreting research results to the public, and providing a scientific basis for the conservation of birds and their habitats.

Studies focus on bird populations and habitats both local and far afield. Many migratory birds whose breeding and wintering grounds are connected by a system of migration stopovers called a flyway, are at risk due to habitat loss and degradation.

In the 1980's PRBO trained hundreds of observers to help survey critical wetlands from Alaska to Baja California and the from the Pacific coast inland to the Great Basin, in order to assess the health of North American shorebirds that migrate in the Pacific Flyway.

Aimed at obtaining the first baseline data on an entire system that supports migratory shorebirds, PRBO's collaborative Pacific Flyway Project showed that that over a million shorebirds rely on San Francisco Bay during the peak spring migration. As a result, the Bay was designated a site of hemispheric importance to shorebirds.

The declining songbird population is being studied in a similar way.

PRBO trains biologists and wildlife managers, in the U.S. and Latin America, to monitor threatened bird populations and thus the health of eco-systems.

PRBO has operated a research and management site for the U.S. Fish and Wildlife Service on the Farallon Islands, 28 miles west of the Golden Gate, for almost 30 years. It helped develop many new management policies like the new gill net fishing regulations that protect the great seabird and marine mammal breeding colonies on these islands.

The group's headquarters for land bird research and public education is at Palomarin Field Station on Mesa Road, Bolinas, at the southern entrance to the Point Reyes National Seashore. Here throughout the year, the public can observe the banding of birds which have been caught in mist nets for monitoring studies.

Bird walks, led by PRBO biologists, are held regularly in West Marin. For more information call (415) 868-1221 or check their web site at http://www.prbo.org

A conservation group that has had a profound effect on the future of West Marin is the Marin Agricultural Land Trust (MALT). It is a non-profit institution which eliminates the development potential of agricultural land by acquiring conservation easements in voluntary transactions with landowners. MALT pays the farmer a sum which equals the amount of reduction in the property's value resulting from the easement restrictions. The landowner retains ownership of the land which can be sold. However the land must remain in agricultural use for perpetuity.

The trust also provides technical information and assistance to landowners on conservation techniques and alternatives, and promotes public awareness of the importance of Marin's agricultural land and the need to preserve it.

MALT organizes hikes and tours of farms, dairies, ranches and vineyards. I went on a MALT hike through Roy's Redwoods to a ridge top with stunning views above San Geronimo Valley. Led by local historian Dewey Livingston, it was interesting (full of historical tidbits) and exciting (we made it back to the road after dark). It passed all my criteria for a good hike with flying colors!

Much of the initial funding for MALT's acquisitions came from $15 million provided by the California Wildlife, Coastal and Park Lands Conservation Bond Initiative passed by California voters in 1988. Other support comes from individuals, foundations and from MALT's 3,600 active members.

MALT continues to work on acquiring easements. It has agricultural conservation easements on 40 Marin Farms and ranches totalling over 26,000 acres. This means 20% of all privately owned agricultural land in the county is protected. For more information on MALT please call 415 663-1158 or write to P. O. Box 809, Point Reyes Station, CA 94956. Their web site is www.malt.org.

NICASIO RESERVOIR AND FARMLAND

FARALLONES MARINE SANCTUARY ASSOCIATION

The newest environmental group playing a role in protecting the natural resources of West Marin is the Farallones Marine Sanctuary Association (FMSA). Established in 1996, FMSA helps the Gulf of the Farallones National Marine Sanctuary fulfill its goal of protecting 948 square nautical miles of water off the California coast west of San Francisco. The sanctuary includes the marine region of the Gulf of the Farallones and the near shore waters of Bodega Bay, Tomales Bay, Estero de San Antonio, Estero Americano and Bolinas

from Drakes Bay to Montara State Beach in San Mateo county in the south.

Another program is SEALS (Sanctuary Education Awareness and Long-term Stewardship) which trains volunteers to conduct baseline, long-term monitoring of harbor seals and human activities in Bolinas Lagoon. SEALS volunteers also educate the public on site in order to minimize disturbance of the harbor seal rookery in Tomales Bay.

The Gulf of the Farallones National Marine Sanc-

FARALLON ISLAND

Bay. FMSA has a program, Beach Watch, which trains volunteers, through 82 hours of classroom and field study, to identify and document dead and live seabirds, marine mammals, and other marine organisms. Volunteers are trained to collect tar balls and other oiled specimens as evidence to be processed in the state's laboratory so that the origin of potentially harmful substances can be traced. Within a few hours of an oil spill in San Francisco Bay in October, 1996, volunteers were out gathering oil samples, contacting animal rescue teams and collecting dead oil fouled birds and data

tuary Visitor Center recently opened at the Old Coast Guard Station, on Crissy Field in the Golden Gate National Recreation Area. It provides visitors with a hands-on interactive experience with nature. They can feel starfish and urchin in a touch tank, see sand dollars and various shells in a sand box and view krill through a microscope. Hours are Wednesday though Sunday, 10 am to 4 pm. For more information on FMSA, please call 415 561-6625 or write to P. O. Box 29386, The Presidio, San Francisco, CA 94129.

BIRD WATCHERS
Olema Valley

Many national parks have associations which raise money for the parks through membership fees and the sale of merchandise. The Point Reyes National Seashore Association, established in 1964, has given over $3 million to its park. The association used these funds for the construction of the Bear Valley Visitor Center and the Clem Miller Education Center. Thousands of Bay Area school children have studied the environment at the education center.

The PRNSA also funded some of the interpretative exhibits at the park's visitor centers and the wayside and trailhead exhibits throughout the park. Other educational programs it finances are the Point Reyes field seminar and the summer science and adventure camps for children. It also funds the park newspaper and projects like the wildlife restoration of the snowy plover and northern elephant seals, the removal of exotic plants, and the rehabilitation of the park after the Mount Vision fire.

To participate in a PRNSA volunteer program or to find out about membership and seminars, please call 415 663-1155 or stop by any Point Reyes visitor center.

TOMALES BAY ASSOCIATION

The Tomales Association is dedicated to preserving and protecting the natural environment of Tomales Bay and its watershed through research, education and active review of conservation and planning issues. It is an all volunteer group with 500 members and no paid officials.

The association originally started in the 60's as a committee of land owners on the east shore of Tomales Bay who were fighting the proposed Marin County plan for massive residential development in their area. In 1970 the TBA opened its membership to homeowners from both sides of the bay and its main goal became preserving the natural beauty of Tomales Bay. In 1979 they were unsuccessfully sued by the Marin Municipal Water District which wanted to increase the size of Kent Lake and divert stream flows away from Lagunitas Creek. This project would have adversely affected the salmon and steelhead run. The TBA now includes any concerned citizen.

Volunteers from the TBA monitor the habitat, coho spawners and juvenile fish in the tributaries of Olema Creek and San Geronimo Creek. They were active in lowering Roy's Dam and its fish ladder a foot and a half to improve the chances of coho salmon and steel-

TIDAL FLOW THROUGH BREAK IN OLD RAIL BED
Tomales Bay

head being able to spawn in upper San Geronimo Creek. With the approval of various government agencies, they plan to make a series of natural looking pools below the dam so that the fish will only have to jump over a two to three foot dam wall. Presently if a fish decides not to use the ladder, they have to jump an eight foot wall. Every season TBA members count the number of fish spawning in the creeks and their tributaries and collect coho carcass tissue samples for analysis by the Bodega Maine Laboratory's DNA study team. They also regularly collect samples of plankton from the bay for the Department of Health Services in an effort to ensure the pristine quality of Tomales Bay.

Working under the non-profit umbrella of the TBA, is Waste Watch, formed when people living on the road to the West Marin Sanitary Landfill noticed increased traffic to the dump. Waste Watch made public a plan to increase the size of the dump. After protests from many local environmental groups, the dump was closed at the end of the summer of 1998.

For more information about these groups, please call 415 663-1467.

LOOKING NORTH FROM KEHOE BLUFFS, 1991
Water color on Arches paper, 14"x10"

KEHOE BEACH, LOOKING SOUTH
Water color on Arches paper, 19"x29"

MCCLURES ROCK
Water color on Arches paper, 19"x29"

THESE ARE paintings by the author, Kathleen Goodwin, done on location and in the studio. She started painting in 1976 when she lost the sight in her right eye. What began as therapy, turned into a lifelong passion. She participates in open studios as well as group and individual shows.

POINT REYES HEADLANDS, 1991
Acrylic on Canvas, 12"x24"

MC CLURES ROCK LOOKING NORTH & SOUTH, 1990
Water color, on three 24" x 42" sheets of Arches paper

POINT REYES BLACK & WHITE PORTFOLIO

POINT REYES HEADLANDS, 1995

LIGHTHOUSE AT POINT BONITA, 1980

BUG EYED HORSE, POINT REYES STATION 1975

FOG FROM MOUNT VISION, 1999

COW CONTEMPLATING THE VOID, 1973

TREES IN FOG, INVERNESS RIDGE, 1992

TREES & LICHEN, OLEMA VALLEY, 1992

COWS & OAK TREE, LUCAS VALLEY ROAD, 1987

TREES IN FOG, DILLON BEACH, 1994

GREAT BEACH IN MOONLIGHT, 1996

CHILDREN'S BEACH, TOMALES BAY, 1980

RICHARD BLAIR is known for his black and white landscapes of Point Reyes. This portfolio is a small sampling of these images. Richard can be spotted sometimes with his head under a black cloth taking pictures with an 8x10" view camera on a wooden tripod. He was park photographer for the National Park Service in Yosemite in the early 1970's. Shooting in Yosemite Valley, where so many great landscape photographers, from Carlton Watkins to Ansel Adams photographed, he learned the possibilities of exposure and development, and the rigors of expressive printmaking. Now he is extending the wet darkroom process to making enlarger exposed duotones which print directly as random dot lithographs on Arches paper.

PUBLISHERS' NOTES

This book is a pioneering project in book publishing. We call it an artisan book because we photographed, wrote, edited, scanned, and designed it as a combined process. Except for running the press and the bindery work, we did it all. Owning the computer and scanning equipment, we were totally free to do what we wanted, without a client, deadline, or publisher. This allowed a rare degree of creative freedom and a tight integration of all the aspects of publishing the book, including marketing. While Kathleen is the author and Richard is the photographer and book designer, we collaborated to the point of exhausted harmony. We are both everywhere in the book. We lugged cameras and scurried when the light was happening. Anecdotes slowly became facts. Learning programs, rebuilding the stupid desktop, just keeping the computers running, and archiving the work were herculean tasks. Desktop computers are barely able to cope with a book of this size. Every step had obstacles. We worked when we had the confidence to proceed. The pay off came when we could visualize and create fearlessly. We hope you will enjoy this book as much as we enjoyed creating it.

ACKNOWLEDGEMENTS

Don Neubacher, John Dell'Osso, Ann Nelson, Dr. Sarah Allen and Lanny Pinola of the National Park Service and Dr. Gary Fellers of the U.S. Geological Survey were invaluable for sharing with us their knowledge of Point Reyes National Seashore and for encouraging us. Annegret Roettchen helped greatly with the initial designs and scans. Peter Koch and Richard Seibert gave us typographic tips. Dr. Rima Blair and Wendy Pritzker assisted in the final editing. Christopher Reesor of Precision Graphics in San Leandro, California kindly let us use his imagesetter at night while Patricia Thorstad patiently showed us its software and mechanics. We also want to thank Mr. Charlie Chan and the staff of Craft Print in Singapore for their hard work. Our late parents, Ponty and Malcom Goodwin and Ann and Hugh E. Blair, were uniquely talented and skilled in ways that provided the foundation we needed to publish this work.

HOW TO ORDER PHOTOGRAPHS

All the images in the book are available as fine art prints. Prices depend on the size of the image, the edition and the print process used; archival black & white, giclée and lithography. We print color images digitally on Fuji Crystal Archive photo paper that lasts between 70 and 120 years. If you see an image you would like as a print, or to use as a stock photo please contact us for price and copyright information. Our address is on the next page.

OPEN STUDIOS AND EVENTS

Open studios is a wonderful way to see artists in their work environment and support their work. We host open studios where we show the public our artwork and sell images both humble and grand. Kind words of encouragement are all that's needed for a visit but you may fall in love with a piece. We present slide shows and discussions on photogaphy and park policy issues. Write or call for studio event information.

WORKSHOPS AND CLASSES

We teach photography and publication art classes. The workshops held in West Marin, combine learning with our incredible environment. They include landscape work at beaches, forests and farms, as well as classes in digital publishing at our studio atop Inverness Ridge. The techniques by which the writing, painting and photographic images become ink on paper are covered. Other printing methods, from silkscreen to digital enlarger printing, are studied. Richard teaches digital imaging from the perspective of 30 years experience in traditional photographic darkrooms, fine art and commercial lithographic platemaking, and experimental printmaking.

COLOPHON

The photography was accomplished with the following cameras; Nikon and Mamiya RZ67 systems, a Fuji panoramic camera, plus Sinar 4x5" and 8x10" view cameras. The film was mostly Fuji Velvia plus some Kodak T-Max 100 and Kodachrome. The text is Caslon 540 Roman and the headline typeface is Bureau Eagle Book. This paper is 150gsm Lumisilk Matt Art paper. It is casebound with Black Saifu Cloth wrapped over 2.5mm board. Endpapers are 150gsm woodfree stock. We scanned from the original camera filmstock with our Dianippon Screen 1015 AI drum scanner into Adobe Photoshop 4.0, where we corrected the color, cleaned and sized the images. The book was designed in Quark Xpress 4.04 on a G-3 Power Macintosh with 320 megs of ram and 13 gigabytes of ultra scsi hard drives. We used an Agfa imagesetter. Retrospect managed the huge backup job of over 50 gigs of images! We burned multiple CD's of chapters as they were created. The positive 175 line films went to Singapore for press proofing. We personally press checked each signature as it was run.

BIBLIOGRAPHY

The Farallon Islands. Sentinels of the Golden Gate by Peter White. Published by Scottwall Associates,San Francisco, 1995
Ranching on the Point Reyes Peninsula. A history of the dairy and beef ranches within Reyes National Seashore,1834-1992 by Dewey Livingston. Published by the National Park Service, Point Reyes Station, Ca, July 1993
The History and Architecture of the Point Reyes Light Station by Dewey Livingston Published by the National Park Service, Point Reyes Station, Ca, 1990
San Francisco's Wilderness Next Door by John Hart, photographs by Richard Sena. Published by Presidio Press, San Rafael, CA, 1979
Tomales Bay/Bodega Bay Watershed Boundary Study published by Point Reyes National Seashore Marin and Sonoma Counties, CA in July 1995
Mount Tamalpais, A History by Lincoln Fairley. Published by Scottwall Associates, San Francisco, 1987
Point Reyes - Secret Places & Magic Moments by Phil Arnot. Published by Wide World Publishing/Tetra P.O.Box 476 San Carlos, CA 94070, 1987
The Natural History of the Point Reyes Peninsula by Jules G. Evens, published by Point Reyes National Seashore Association, Point Reyes, CA 94956, 1988
The Wilder Shore by Morley Baer and David Rain Wallace published by Sierra Club Books, 1984
California Coastal Resource Guide published by the University of California Press copyright California Coastal Commission, 1987
Herons & Egrets of Audubon Canyon Ranch by Helen Pratt, published by Helen Pratt, 1993
Farming on the Edge by John Hart, published by the University of California Press, Berkeley, 1990

CONTACTING COLOR & LIGHT EDITIONS

Color & Light Editions
P.O. Box 934
Point Reyes Station, CA 94956

www.pointreyesvisions.com
www.richardblair.com

Kathleen Goodwin's web pages are linked to the Point Reyes Visions website.

e-mail: kathrich@svn.net

Call 415 663-1615 for additional signed copies of *Point Reyes Vision*s or to be put on the mailing list. We welcome your comments and interest.